Latinidad and Film

Dania Abreu-Torres
Rosana Blanco-Cano • Rita E. Urquijo-Ruiz

Latinidad and Film

Queer and Feminist Cinema in the Americas

With the special contribution of Henriette Korthals Altes,
Cindi Marín, and Megan Medrano

Dania Abreu-Torres
Trinity University
San Antonio, TX, USA

Rosana Blanco-Cano
Trinity University
San Antonio, TX, USA

Rita E. Urquijo-Ruiz
Trinity University
San Antonio, TX, USA

ISBN 978-3-031-56117-7   ISBN 978-3-031-56118-4   (eBook)
https://doi.org/10.1007/978-3-031-56118-4

© The Editor(s) (if applicable) and The Author(s), under exclusive license to Springer Nature Switzerland AG 2024
This work is subject to copyright. All rights are solely and exclusively licensed by the Publisher, whether the whole or part of the material is concerned, specifically the rights of translation, reprinting, reuse of illustrations, recitation, broadcasting, reproduction on microfilms or in any other physical way, and transmission or information storage and retrieval, electronic adaptation, computer software, or by similar or dissimilar methodology now known or hereafter developed.
The use of general descriptive names, registered names, trademarks, service marks, etc. in this publication does not imply, even in the absence of a specific statement, that such names are exempt from the relevant protective laws and regulations and therefore free for general use.
The publisher, the authors and the editors are safe to assume that the advice and information in this book are believed to be true and accurate at the date of publication. Neither the publisher nor the authors or the editors give a warranty, expressed or implied, with respect to the material contained herein or for any errors or omissions that may have been made. The publisher remains neutral with regard to jurisdictional claims in published maps and institutional affiliations.

This Palgrave Macmillan imprint is published by the registered company Springer Nature Switzerland AG.
The registered company address is: Gewerbestrasse 11, 6330 Cham, Switzerland

Paper in this product is recyclable.

Preface

In the film *Danzón*, the main character, Julia, arrives in Veracruz in search of her dance partner. With suitcases in hand, she walks with confidence out of the train station, looking ahead, as if understanding that whatever situation she will face, she will do so on her own. Through a panoramic gaze, the director of the film, María Novaro, affirms Julia's confidence by showing multiple men looking at her body as she is passing by. Instead of framing Julia through a male, voyeuristic point of view, Novaro shifts the patriarchal gaze and transforms her film into a reclamation of her protagonist's independence and agency. This book's objectives are formulated around such female and queer agencies and aim to shift how we, students, faculty, and the general public, watch and understand U.S. Latinx and Latin American films.

Latinidad and Film: Queer and Feminist Cinema in the Americas presents a series of films that have not been analyzed in depth before and, in some cases, have not reached wide distribution, being limited to screenings at festivals and special events. These films, however, have been thresholds on how U.S. Latinx, Latin American, and Caribbean histories have moved from heteronormative patriarchal discourses to more gender-inclusive ones. All chapters feature directors that have allied themselves with new strategies to represent families, queer individuals, the home, and the women/people that manage the domestic and public spaces they inhabit. Most of the directors are women whose mission is to portray womanhood in all its aspects, the negative and the positive, as they offer alternatives to gender relations. We hope that the 11 films included not only foster discussions about history, sexuality, and gender politics but also conversations about representation, the precarious situation of the film industry for Latinx and Latin American directors, in Latin America, the United States, and the Caribbean, as well as the need for a better international and U.S. distribution of these groundbreaking films.

We, the co-authors of this book, have been working on this manuscript since 2017 when Diana Chavarría, Cindi Marín, and Megan Medrano, three brilliant students in our Latin American film studies courses, accepted to collaborate with us on a project as part of the Summer Undergraduate Research Fellowship (SURF) from the Mellon Initiative at Trinity University. Since then, the project has taken many forms and included a variation of films and analyses. The pandemic in 2020 halted our efforts and the work we had achieved at that time but also allowed for space to reframe our theories, rethink the logistics of the films included, and define our target audiences. This book is intended for undergraduate and graduate students who would like to learn more about U.S. Latinx, Latin American, and Caribbean films in the periphery of what may be called the Latinx/Latin American film canon; for the faculty that teach film courses so they have a companion that would allow for deeper conversations with their students; and for the general public so that by reading about these films they can have a sense of how they portray and represent particular stories centered around family and gender expectations that have changed through time and in relationship with the United States and Hollywood.

This book would not have been possible without the support of the Mellon Initiative at Trinity University, the Department of Modern Languages and Literatures, and the special contribution of our students Diana, Cindi, and Megan. They provided some of the foundational work and analyses in various chapters and we are forever grateful and proud of their contributions. They, like Julia in *Danzón*, helped us to confidently navigate the challenging path of writing this book and to look forward to its completion.

San Antonio, TX, USA	Dania Abreu-Torres
San Antonio, TX, USA	Rosana Blanco-Cano
San Antonio, TX, USA	Rita E. Urquijo-Ruiz

Contents

Part I	Breaking the Mold	1
1	*Danzón* (María Novaro, 1991, Mexico/Spain)	3
2	*Brincando el Charco: Portrait of a Puerto Rican* (Frances Negrón-Muntaner. 1994, U.S./Puerto Rico)	15
Part II	Anxieties and Sexualities	27
3	*Tan de Repente* (Diego Lerman. 2002, Argentina)	29
4	*Madeinusa* (Claudia Llosa. 2006, Perú)	41
5	*Qué Tan Lejos* (Tania Hermida. 2006, Ecuador)	51
Part III	Breaking the Binary	63
6	*La Mission* (Peter Bratt, 2009, USA)	65
7	*Entre Nos* (Paola Mendoza and Gloria La Morte. 2009, USA)	73

8 *La Hija Natural* (Dir. Leticia Tonos. 2011, República Dominicana)   85

Part IV   Depatriarchalizing   99

9 *Mosquita y Mari* (Aurora Guerrero. 2012, USA)   101

10 *Pelo Malo* (Mariana Rondón. 2013, Venezuela)   113

11 *Bruising for Besos* (Adelina Anthony, 2016, USA)   127

Index   141

LIST OF FIGURES

Fig. 1.1	Julia and Susy dancing danzón	9
Fig. 3.1	Marcia receives an offer from Mao and Lenin	32
Fig. 5.1	Esperanza and Tristeza traveling together	52
Fig. 7.1	Gabriel, Mariana, and Andrea	75
Fig. 9.1	*Mari y Mosquita* bonding	103
Fig. 11.1	Daña and Yoli meet	135

Introduction

Latin American cinema has provided a consistent influence on international filmography and cinematic movements since the mid-twentieth century. The Golden Age of Mexican Cinema (1930–1960), the Brazilian Cinema Novo (1960 and 1970), and the Cuban revolutionary films during the 1960s, as well as other creators and contributors, have inspired multiple studies that have evidenced the impact of this cinema. Presently, however, research regarding sexuality and gender issues especially focused on Latin American women and LGBTQ+ directors is minimal. This book, *Latinidad and Film: Queer and Feminist Cinema in the Americas*, examines a total of 11 contemporary Latin American and U.S. Latinx films that critically deal with gender and sexuality, emphasizing the underexplored perspectives of women directors and queer (LGBTQ+) cinematic identities in the twentieth and twenty-first centuries. Through a close examination of these films, we reflect on how such productions critically offer cultural discourses that either prevent or enable agency for women within the Latin American and U.S. Latinx contemporary film industries. In addition, we closely examine cinematic styles that break with traditional heteronormative and/or male-centric visual conventions, thus proposing that cinema, through innovative visual language, is empowering these groups and communities that historically have been excluded from mainstream films. For this analysis, we want to adopt the definition of queerness proposed by Venkatesh: we want to make visible films that are devoted to the "unpack[ing] of heteronormative politics and subjectivities" (22), thus evidencing those discourses as cultural and therefore, malleable. As Venkatesh proposes as well, it is urgent to make visible films that are creating empathy toward the queer characters and stories for the simple and yet important fact of humanizing queer identities. At the same time, it is urgent to open new spaces of discursive power in society. *Latinidad and Film* provides the readers with a unique perspective by examining and creating analytical dialogues with productions that come from the margins of Latin American industries as well. Historically, places like Mexico, Argentina, and Brazil have been the main centers of film production. This book, however, is an explorative attempt to make visible the Latinx/Latin American cinema from other countries: Ecuador, Puerto Rico, Venezuela, Dominican Republic, among others. The 11 films examined cover a broad array of cinematic perspectives and styles from the 1990s to 2016. At the same time, the analysis considers cinema as a cultural artifact, in which meaning and visual representations may depend on a specific context, either socio-historical, economic, or political, and that cultural practices and discourses can be debunked such as patriarchal oppression and homophobia in Latinx/Latin American identities.

Patriarchy, according to Julieta Paredes, is that discourse that not only oppresses women but that represents all the exploitations (of gender, race, representation, and economic oppression) that have marked our modern times (1). In order to be liberated from it, cultural producers, as a community, must "depatriarchalize" (*despatriarcalizar*) spaces and representations in which stereotypes and limiting social conventions have been the customary ways to create an idea of Latin America and the U.S. Latinx cultures to the world. The cinematic productions considered in this book subvert these patriarchal discourses by disarming the stereotypes, questioning such conventions, and leading new figures that will rewrite how Latin American and U.S. Latinx societies and their political and economic systems are represented through the reconfiguration of the family and its gender roles contained within limiting social institutions.

Historically, the patriarchal and heterosexist institution of the family has been the allegorical representation of the nation in Latin America and beyond. Often, this allegory is related to the discourse of mestizaje, the ideal biological possibility of the union of a European man with an Indigenous woman. Casta paintings ["cuadros de castas"] in Mexico and Peru are the perfect examples of this biological discourse and how it is transformed into a political and economic ideology by creating a functional, racial, and gender hierarchy. *Latinidad and Film* confronts these nationalist discourses and hierarchies by bringing the points of view of women and LGBTQ+ directors on how families and the national allegory around them are much more diverse and complex than the traditional heterosexual family representation. In the films examined in this book, father figures are mostly absent, girls explore the streets to find alternatives out of social and gender expectations, boys are inscribed in the domestic sphere and discover new forms of gender identity, and mothers are more complex than the virginal and sacrificial figures often associated with them. We aim to highlight the complexities and nuances of Latin American, Caribbean, and U.S. Latinx cinema in order to present alternatives and new modes of creating families and, therefore, communities that go beyond the national, heteronormative construct. We intend to present a more contemporary and exhaustive analysis of the films by proposing not only close readings of the productions but also paying specific attention to the discursive and visual components of the films (plot, characters, setting) as well as also considering the external elements that influence the creative process involved in filmmaking (the director's background and context, participant producers, and the cinematographer's point of view). The stories in front and behind the cameras portray women and/or queer individuals that are constantly challenging patriarchal and heteronormative discourses in the U.S. Latinx and Latin American communities. These films are queering the Latin American and U.S. Latinx cinema industry by creating non-conformist gender narratives, styles, and characters that enable spectators to go beyond the "safe distance" (Venkatesh 26) in relation to film and be more empathic toward the multiple struggles that women and the LGBTQ+ community still experience in the contexts that we are analyzing.

Latinidad and Film is organized into four main parts that emphasize the type of cultural subversion that each film presents: Breaking the Mold; Anxieties and Sexualities; Breaking the Binary; and Depatriarchalizing. Below we offer a brief description of each section and its films as a way to guide the reader to the main principles of the analysis and to provide an overview of the subsequent chapters.

Part I: Breaking the Mold

The films by women directors in the 1990s were a response to the dominant patriarchal oppression, women's sexualization, and the family and romantic relationships that most of the 1980s films portrayed. The films in this section represent an exploration of how to break the heteropatriarchal mold and include other discourses on cinematic representation, particularly as part of national discourses and the standardization of gender conventions.

1. *Danzón (Mexico, María Novaro, 1991)*
   Besides providing a reflection on Novaro's prolific career, the first section of the chapter analyzes how her film *Danzón* can be read as transitional: one that exemplifies the changes to the cinematic production laws that enabled new ways of producing film in Mexico in the 1990s. In this sense, the chapter also explores how *Danzón* connects nostalgic discourses on Mexican identity from the Golden Age of Mexican Cinema, with a reflexive perspective that centers on the importance of social, cultural, and economic agency for women in contemporary Mexico. Through the examined aspects, the chapter critically reflects on visual resources that Novaro uses in her film to depict the evolution of her protagonist who starts following the very strict norms of danzón and Mexican society but who later becomes a more independent dancer who also decides the direction of her own life and how she lives sexually and owns her body.
2. *Brincando el Charco (the United States, Mainland and Puerto Rico, Frances Negrón-Muntaner, 1994)*
   Frances Negrón-Muntaner's film is considered an experimental experience of queerness and national identity, while also intersecting it with racial discourses in the Puerto Rican national imaginary. *Brincando el Charco* deconstructs and reconstructs Puerto Rican identity by questioning its basic performance premise: the family. Each member has a specific gender role and the main character, Claudia, does not follow the one assigned to her. She is a lesbian and her definition of national identity is completely different from what is expected from her. Although the material may provide for a melodramatic perspective, Negrón-Muntaner breaks with this approach by focusing on reflections about her different experiences with Puerto Rican and other diverse communities in Philadelphia. The "history" represented in the film is fragmented, interrupted, and artificial as any other cultural production, but it has a conscience of artificiality that allows the spectator to trace a new kind of national identity, queering the national performance in a hopeful light for inclusion.

Part II: Anxieties and Sexualities

After breaking the mold on how women and the LGBTQ+ community should be considered in the discussions of national discourses, the films in this section further the exploration of the individuals in the collective and manifest their anxieties of belonging. Sexuality, both as a chosen and active engagement, is redefined and consistently questioned, moving the filmmakers to negotiate and propose new standards of sexual engagement, activity, and psychological resilience.

3. *Tan de Repente (Argentina, Diego Lerman, 2002)*
   An internationally co-produced film, Diego Lerman's opera prima, *Tan de Repente* (2002), is directly connected to the so-called New Argentine Film by portraying a gray image of Buenos Aires and its inhabitants. In addition to analyzing some of the main features in Lerman's oeuvre, the chapter centers on three moments in which the status quo and its corresponding inertia are shattered, presenting, both visually and discoursively, innovative approaches to the concept of relationships, love, desire, and the notion of happiness. The everyday life of a young working-class woman is disrupted through the actions of the two protagonists: two young lesbians who live their lives on the margins of what is considered acceptable. This black-and-white film proves to have a complex repertoire of emotions that break with traditional conventions of representation, allowing the spectators to contemplate other ways of defining the female and lesbian identity in post-crisis Argentina.

4. *Madeinusa (Peru, Claudia Llosa, 2006)*
   As a powerful but controversial film, *Madeinusa* is a portrayal of an Indigenous community that questions the interactions of power and gender. The chapter analyzes how Llosa constructs a strong female character in a dystopian circumstance that dialogues with the Indigenous community's realities from which it is inspired. Corruption, sexual abuse, and sexual freedom are some of the themes exposed in the film and in which Madeinusa, the protagonist, thrives, as she is able to manipulate the desires of others to fulfill her own. The focus on the religious environment in which the storyline is developed emphasizes the breaking of the conventional rules of modesty and conservatism by imagining a god that turns his back on his children so they can play in absolute freedom as they

break all social and familial contracts. Freedom, then, is what is desired by Madeinusa and what she pursues without regrets.

5. *Qué Tan Lejos (Ecuador, Tania Hermida, 2006)*
An innovative take on the road movie genre, *Qué Tan Lejos* portrays the relationship between two women with opposite personalities, Tristeza (Sadness) and Esperanza (Hope), while traveling. The chapter's objective is to analyze how Tania Hermida recreates the road movie not only as a genre in which growth and maturity are achieved by the characters but also as a genre in which gender solidarity is explored. The solidification of the solidarity between these women develops without any male love interests in sight. Although Tristeza's travel is motivated by a man (she wants to stop her ex-boyfriend's wedding), Hermida's perspective on women moves them beyond the "whys" to focus on the "how" and their discoveries. Her conversations are political, tender, and nostalgic, providing the protagonists with a space to define themselves by their own company.

Part III: Breaking the Binary

New types of representational figures begin to break through in this section's film selection. After exploring the anxieties of alternative modes of sexuality and gender performance, the characters in these films expose the fissures of gender conventions and reclaim their own discursive versions. They recreate their own histories and craft better representations of themselves, different from those offered by previous generations in each of their countries. These new versions are not smoothly recreated but constructed as part of the struggles to break the old heteropatriarchal mold in order to move beyond the binary into new paths of more fluid and negotiated gender performances.

6. *La Mission (the United States, Peter Bratt, 2009)*
This chapter examines Peter Bratt's *La Mission* which proposes a thorough reflection on one of the most complex aspects of Latinx cultures: the multiple and somewhat contradictory definitions of masculinity. This analysis includes some of the traits in Bratt's independent cinematic production such as the economic and social struggles of today's Latinx communities in the United States, the use of intersectionality as a filmmaking approach, and the impact of the director's personal experience in the development of a cinema that speaks from the margins. The chapter highlights the discursive

and visual resources utilized to ponder the constraining definitions of masculinity that traditionally have been present in U.S. Latinx communities. In this sense, the film challenges not only the use of violence as domination, the behaviors that assert an individual as masculine, as well as the discourses and practices that have oppressed those who break with the heterosexual compulsion historically associated with the U.S. Latinx experience.

7. *Entre Nos (the United States, Colombia. Gloria La Morte and Paola Mendoza, 2009)*
   Entre Nos is the personal portrayal of a Colombian immigrant family struggling to survive in New York City. Based on the experiences of Paola Mendoza (co-director with Gloria La Morte) the film is an intimate representation of Mariana, a woman who becomes empowered and resilient, after her husband abandons her shortly after arriving in the United States. With a tourist visa that will soon expire, Mariana's possibilities for employment are limited and become nulled when her husband leaves her and their two children. She must overcome the emotional and physical abandonment by being strong for her children, being creative with their financial limitations as a family, and focusing on the positive aspects of life as they navigate their challenging new world. The aspects analyzed in this chapter synthesize Mendoza and La Morte's vision of this particular story of strength and resiliency via a personal gaze that explores an immigrant woman's story of survival.

8. *La Hija Natural (Dominican Republic, Leticia Tonos, 2011)*
   Set in a rural area of the Dominican Republic, this film is not a representation of the patriarchal presence on the island, a common portrayal in many Dominican films. What Leticia Tonos achieved with this film is to delicately disarm this heteropatriarchal discourse through her character Maria. The analysis demonstrates this patriarchal disarming by describing how Tonos' direction is influenced by quotidian situations that marvelously transform her characters. Searching for her father, Maria confronts her fears and learns more about her lost mother. She becomes a woman on her own terms, creating a safe space where she is able to reconcile with her father. Manhood is questioned through humor; womanhood is developed through survival. By creating a masculine crisis and a thriving female character, Tonos is subverting the patriarchal narrative without condemning one side or the other.

Part IV: Depatriarchalizing

Following Julieta Paredes' conceptualization of the need to "despatriarcalizar," the films in this section completely break with the heteropatriarchy and its mode of control still present in previous representations. These directors bring new perspectives where gender is (re)constructed in (trans)national discourses. In these films, women are no longer the victims. They are proactive agents of their stories who do not need to define themselves. These protagonists are complex characters who are not limited to their gender roles as they constantly create and redefine their own hopeful identities.

9. *Mosquita y Mari (the United States, Aurora Guerrero, 2012)*
   This film by Aurora Guerrero focuses on the relationship and friendship of two young Chicanas: Yolanda (Mosquita) and Mari. As a traditional coming-of-age story, the film follows the young women, their struggles in school, with friends, and, particularly, their struggles with their parents, while they start relying on each other a little more intimately as they become best friends. Although the film does not conclude with a coming-out story, Yolanda's exploration of new opportunities via her friendship with Mari expands through the director's queer gaze. Their relationship is treated not as an anomaly, as heteronormative conventions try to define the LGBTQ+ experience, but as part of discovering oneself. This intimacy between Yolanda and Mari is analyzed through the perspective of a coming-of-age story in a Latinx community with its specific cultural expectations and education—particularly for the studious Yolanda; the impact of family on the decisions these young women (and any Latina) must confront in order to be successful; and how identity and sexuality are interrelated with the cultural expectations and family influence on self-discovery and a potential future. Guerrero does not offer a strong political statement but a quotidian, tender gaze on these young Chicanas and how they learn to navigate the complex community in which they live.

10. *Pelo Malo (Venezuela, Mariana Rondón, 2013)*
    Mariana Rondón sets her successful film *Pelo Malo* in the heart of the city of Caracas, Venezuela. The country is suffering the health crisis of its then-authoritarian president Hugo Chávez, serving as a

background to another crisis, one more individual and intimate. While "Chavismo" helped create a nationalism that affected gender activism, allowing more women to participate in the national guard and local police forces, it also profoundly ingrained authoritarian masculinity that pushed a new female workforce to the margins when the crisis began and work started to become scarce. This chapter analyzes how this socio-political context affects the lives of Martha and Junior, the family at the center of this film. The aspects analyzed focus on the construction of Junior's queer identity and how Martha reacts to it and on approaches that demonstrate Rondón's goal to offer a different reading of family, gender identification, and the social pressures that stifle any identity development.

11. *Bruising for Besos (the United States, AdeRisa Productions, Adelina Anthony, 2016)*
    In her debut and independently produced film *Bruising for Besos*, Xicana queer writer, actor, director, and producer Adelina Anthony plays the role of the protagonist, Yoli Villamontes, who confronts present and past domestic violence as she attempts to "build familia from scratch" with other queer and trans people of color in Los Angeles, California. Yoli, a Xicana jota (queer) originally from Texas, has left her biological family behind to pursue her art in California. Anthony names her after "Yolotl" (the word for "heart" in Nahuatl) because Yoli travels through life with a giving and open heart that betrays her as she falls into a physically abusive relationship with her Puerto Rican lover Daña (a name which translates as someone who hurts others). This relationship replicates the violent episodes from Yoli's parents that traumatized her as a small child. This chapter focuses on a survivor of Latinx queer domestic and intimate partner violence, on Xicana queer Indigenous identity, and art as healing. Anthony takes advantage of her decades of experience in theater and performance as she offers her masterful directorial debut in what promises to be the first of a series of films by AdeRisa Productions, a company she co-founded with her partner, Marisa Becerra.

An Invitation and Our Hope

As an explorative attempt to contribute toward the visibility of women and queer filmmakers, we invite other scholars to continue exploring U.S. Latinx and Latin American cinema from the margins. In our case, this book has been the result of undergraduate classes and discussions that we had among ourselves. In this sense, Diana Chavarría, Cindi Marín, and Megan Medrano, three former students, helped with the initial examination of some chapters by participating in one of our Latin American Cinema classes during a semester and later collaborating with us on a Mellon Summer Institute sponsored by the Mellon Initiative at Trinity University. These students are special contributors to this book. Our overall objective has been to provide an inclusive dialogue that suggests a framework that can further discussions regarding gender studies, LGBTQ+ discourses, and national identities in U.S. Latinx and Latin American communities that will inform and benefit discussions in the classroom as well as in the public arena. We hope this project encourages more publications specifically focused on these critical topics that challenge, analyze, and demand equality in a worldwide environment that is constantly moving toward the consolidation of repressive, regressive, and discriminatory laws and practices against women, (im)migrants, queer, Latinx, Afro-Latinx, and other communities of color that inhabit the margins of capitalist societies across the Americas.

Works Cited

Paredes, Julieta. "Despatriarcalización: Una respuesta categórica del feminismo comunitario (descolonizando la vida)." *Bolivian Studies Journal/Revista de Estudios Bolivianos*, vol. 21, 2015, pp. 100–115. DOI: https://doi.org/10.5195/bsj.2015.144.

Venketash, Vinodh. *New Maricón Cinema*. University of Texas Press, 2016.

PART I

Breaking the Mold

CHAPTER 1

Danzón (María Novaro, 1991, Mexico/Spain)

Abstract Besides providing a reflection on Novaro's prolific career, the first section of the chapter analyzes how her film *Danzón* can be read as transitional one that exemplifies the changes to the cinematic production laws that enabled new ways of producing film in Mexico in the 1990s. In this sense, the chapter also explores how *Danzón* connects nostalgic discourses on Mexican identity from the Golden Age of Mexican Cinema, with a reflexive perspective that centers on the importance of social, cultural, and economic agency for women in contemporary Mexico. Through the examined aspects, the chapter critically reflects on visual resources that Novaro uses in her film to depict the evolution of her protagonist who starts following the very strict norms of danzón and Mexican society but who later becomes a more independent dancer who also decides the direction of her own life and how she lives sexually and owns her body.

Keywords Gender roles • Self-discovery • Independence • Mexican cinema • Womanhood

Production

Production:	Instituto Mexicano de Cinematografía (IMCINE), Fondo de Fomento a la Calidad Cinematográfica, Gobierno del Estado de Veracruz, Macondo Cine Video, Tabasco Films [México]; Televisión Española (TVE)
Director	María Novaro
Screenwriters	Beatriz Novaro and María Novaro
Director of Photography	Rodrigo García
Editing	Nelson Rodríguez and María Novaro

Cast

María Rojo	Julia Solórzano
Carmen Salinas	Doña Ti
Tito Vasconcelos	Susy
Margarita Isabel	Silvia
Víctor Carpinteiro	Rubén
Cheli Godínez	Tere
Daniel Rergis	Carmelo Benítez
Adyari Chazaro	Perla
Blanca Guerra	La Colorada

Synopsis

Julia, a phone operator in Mexico City and a single mother, has a strong passion for danzón. Every Wednesday, she and her friend Silvia dance at the "Salón de baile Colonia." Julia has danced with the same danzón partner, Carmelo, for more than seven years. One day, he disappears and she decides to go find him, traveling to the coastal area of the state of Veracruz. Instead of finding Carmelo, however, she takes the opportunity to experience new adventures from which she will become aware of her personal needs and desires.

Director's Take: María Novaro (1951–)

María Novaro is one of the most renowned women filmmakers in Mexico. She began her career in film in the 1970s, by becoming a member of the Colectivo Cine-Mujer. Participating in the collective inspired Novaro to pursue a formal career in film production after attending the *Centro*

Universitario de Estudios Cinematográficos/University Center for Cinematographic Studies (CUEC) at Mexico's National University. As a film production student, she developed a series of shorts (in Super 8 and 16 mm format). An example of this early cinematic production is *Una isla rodeada de agua* (*An Island Surrounded by Water*, 1985). In this short, she already includes some of the most notable characteristics of her cinematic universe: the experience of being a woman in contemporary Mexico, the intersection of race, gender, class, and sexual orientation in the creation of identities such as motherhood, among others. Aesthetically, and even though this is a low-budget production, the short also presents her personalized approach with the camera, creating a point of view that breaks with the traditional cinematic language that historically has objectified women's bodies on the screen. In Novaro's universe, it is necessary to use the plots and technical features to create strong characters who are protagonists of their own lives and who own their bodies. Even though it is possible to recognize her cinematic style and tone throughout her prolific career, each one of her films is singular, considering, respectively, the historical and temporary values that mark the experience of the diverse array of female characters she has created for over two decades. Thus, Novaro's current productions propose an acute examination of the multiple circumstances that Mexican women can experience throughout their lives. Her female characters will claim their recognition of their cultural citizenship, deciding, even against all odds, the direction of their own lives. Without renouncing love, in most of the cases within the heterosexual matrix, the strong female characters in all her films—*Lola* (1989), *Danzón* (1991), *El jardín del edén* [*The Garden of Eden*] (1994), *Sin dejar huella* [*Leaving No Trace*] (2000), and *Las buenas hierbas* [*The Good Herbs*] (2008)—abandon their comfort zones to explore unknown, and sometimes more fulfilling, aspects of their personal expression. *Danzón*, in particular, is considered a pivotal film for Latin American women's directors of the twentieth century and beyond.

Commentary and Context

During the 1990s, Mexican cinema was able to undergo a "rebirth" after decades of dependence on the subsidies and grants provided by the government. In agreement with the neoliberal initiatives consolidated by Carlos Salinas de Gortari's regime, a new law of cinematic co-production was approved in 1992, enabling collaborations between the private and the public sectors, and bringing to the table the possibility of co-producing cinema with foreign organizations. This new production formula resulted in better quality films, also opening Mexican cinema to a more reliable and effective system of distribution. In addition, liberating cinema from governmental support facilitated new ways of narrating and conceiving discourses on Mexican identity and, as a consequence, on gender discourses and practices. Since the 1990s, this new era of cinematic production in Mexico has enabled the exploration of topics that were considered taboo. In a sense, and as Novaro demonstrates through her prolific oeuvre, the cinematic screen has finally become a cultural space that critically and openly reflects on social and cultural transformations.

Disidentifying from the patronizing role that the government played for decades, Mexican filmmakers cleverly dislocated the controlled image of the *gran familia mexicana* [the great Mexican family], which for many decades was portrayed as stable, and in correspondence with the cultural imaginary that perpetuated the role of the father as a direct representative of the Catholic church and/or governmental authority within the domestic space. Novaro's families lack the patriarchal figures overexploited through the Golden Age of Mexican Cinema. The contours of the heteronormative family are disrupted with the development of female protagonists who are independent women, who actively participate both in the public and private spaces. From the 1980s to the present, Novaro critically discusses practices and discourses that permeate traditional definitions of Mexican identity in relation to genre and gender. With her films, she proposes a variety of experiences within the complex geographical map in which her characters operate. With her stories and cinematographic style, it is possible to further understand the multiple ways in which excluded groups—women, Indigenous people, and the LBGTQ+ communities—intervene to claim their recognition as citizens in contemporary Mexico.

It could be argued that *Danzón* is the most representative film in Novaro's prolific cinematic production. Co-produced by Mexican and Spanish funding, this film proposes, as the director indicated in an interview with Santiago Tabernero (2011), a space to further reflect on the sociocultural changes that Mexico experienced as a society during the second half of the twentieth century. In this sense, the film cleverly depicts a nostalgic tone that contrasts with the subtle transgressions associated with the behavior of the protagonist. Through the use of music, dance, and cultural performance, all enacted in emblematic spaces such as the *salones de baile* [dance halls], Novaro connects the sentimental education of post-revolutionary Mexico with the profound social transformations that occurred from the 1950s to the 1970s. In *Danzón*, México is depicted as an evolving geography where social, political, and cultural movements—such as the 1950s railway unionizing efforts, the 1968 students' movement, the literary and musical counterculture, the consolidation of the feminist and LGBTQ+ movements—dramatically impacted the definitions of cultural identity, clearly reshaping the status of women, and other historically marginalized groups. In this sense, women increased their participation in the cultural and artistic spheres, especially in film, proposing new symbolic meanings in relation to the experiences of gender and sexuality. Novaro's work, clearly framed under those decades of change, links the old and the new ways of producing cinema in Mexico. Through her complex visual style and powerful script, it is possible to identify elements created in the Golden Age of Mexican Cinema, the experimental cinemas from the 1960s and 1970s, and her own cinematic language that breaks with traditional logic of representation, particularly those that concern the representation of the female body. Films like *Danzón* clearly hinge on a nostalgic relationship with the past—actively represented through the use of music in juxtaposition with mythical geographical spaces in the Mexican imagery—with the changing reality of Mexico City in the early 1990s.

Co-written by Novaro and her sister, Beatriz Novaro, this film cleverly introduces a fresh and almost absent perspective in Mexican cinema. *Danzón* not only comes from the imagination of two talented female cultural producers, the Novaro sisters, but also represents, like very few cinematic productions, everyday life as well as the dreams and fears of working-class Mexican women. Julia Solórzano, the protagonist, transforms from an idealized version of Mexicanness, (the demure woman who clearly knows her role in danzón, an evocative musical tune) into a more nuanced version of her identity, an aspect that has been historically absent from the Mexican cinematic screens. She, a single and independent mother, embodies a "hinge" identity, freely circulating through the streets of both Mexico City and the port of Veracruz, dislocating with her mobility and movements the static national model of the suffering woman and mother. The ambiguous yet rich nature of Julia is also characteristic, as Amy Sutherland proposes, of the visual and narrative elements that constitute the film. Sutherland argues that it is impossible to classify *Danzón* under one specific category. While the film depicts a complex female character, who cleverly goes beyond the stereotypical binary equation that defined womanhood during the Golden Age of Mexican Cinema—the virginal mother versus the fallen woman—it is difficult to say that the film adopts a feminist stance that would openly criticize the patriarchal structures that still limit the position of working-class women in Mexico.

What is particularly unique about this production is that it opens the door to recognizing some of the cultural elements that intervene in the definition of Mexican sentimental education, using, at the same time, visual markers that propose an homage to the Golden Age of Mexican Cinema—the music, colors, social attitudes. More than proposing a simple and nostalgic cinematic production, however, Novaro is able to subvert some of these cultural markers by proposing intimate transformations in her female characters. At the beginning of the film, the main character, Julia, seems to accept a traditional order when dancing and participating in other everyday activities. She is used to living an ordered life in which the male figure leads and controls the movements of his female counterpart. Nevertheless, the physical and affective displacements that the main character experiences enable her to transform herself into the leader not only of her own life but also of her attitude and assertiveness as a danzón dancer.

"Teach Me to Dance as a Woman, for Me to be Able to Understand You [Enséñame como mujer para que te entienda]"

In Novaro's filmic production, there is a specific concern that the filmmaker discusses throughout her productions: What is the meaning of "vivir-se" [to allow oneself to live freely and passionately] as a woman or as a man? In her first feature film, *Lola* (1989), the story serves as a means for denouncing some of the oppressive cultural dynamics that still operate to control the experience of women, particularly those who are mothers. In *Danzón*, the critical perspective is even more complex since the film not only denounces traditional gendered discourses and practices through a comedic tone but also reflects on the cultural construction of such limiting social scripts. In that sense, *Danzón* makes explicit that constructs around gender and sexuality are not "natural" but culturally defined in specific geographies and temporalities. Given their temporal and cultural constitution, they can also be transformed to propose more democratic definitions of sexual and gender identities (Fig. 1.1).

In *Danzón*, the cinematic gaze distances itself from the traditional androcentric and Euro-centric points of view that usually position women, people of color, and other alternative identities on the margins. Thus, the film opens new expressive spaces for those individuals who have been

Fig. 1.1 Julia and Susy dancing danzón

historically silenced for not representing the ideal notion of citizenship. Novaro is interested in representing the voice and experience of working-class women, prostitutes, LGBTQ+ communities, and Indigenous people, among other marginal individuals. Therefore, it is not by chance that Julia's accomplice in her search for her personal transformation is Susy, a transgender character who openly talks about her own female subjectivity. Having a solo drag queen show at a local bar, Susy's preparation routine and performance demonstrate that gender identity is constructed through a series of sophisticated techniques (make-up, body language, clothes) that are used repeatedly in everyday life or in more extraordinary events like in the show where she carefully performs. As Romy Sutherland suggests, Novaro presents in *Danzón* the complexity and ambiguity of gender, breaking not only with the discourses that have historically defined and regulated women's lives in Mexico (virgin/whore) but also the basic definitions of what is considered masculine and feminine. Susy is an expert in becoming a "woman" for her show and, at times, for her everyday life; her corporeality appears "feminine," and she clearly defines herself as a woman. When Julia meets Susy, her traditional notions of gender identity and performance are shaken. Susy's flexibility and her honest conversations about her identity serve as an ideal method for Julia to also question the limits of her own self.

Susy is a lively character, who invites her, throughout various moments in the story, to experience new ways of being. Julia tries on new fashion styles—more expressive—and also explores with Susy new ways of dancing to her favorite music: danzón. One of the most emblematic scenes of this film is the one in which Susy asks Julia to teach her how to dance danzón. Despite the fact that Susy is only wearing shorts and a top tank, evoking a non-feminine outfit, she refuses to adopt the position of the man when dancing. At first, Julia gives Susy instructions on how to position the arms and other "sacred" principles of "danzón cerrado," indicating that the dancers must abide by those rules to get the "beautiful aspects" (lo bonito) of her favorite music style. Susy, however, does not know how to follow Julia's instructions: "hold me as a man; hold me in such a way that I feel your fingers dictating to me what to do." The heteronormative equation, and its dynamics of power, is not appealing for Susy. She clearly states that she wants to learn the women's steps for her to be able to understand ["enséñame como mujer, para que te entienda"]. This is a watershed moment for the protagonist. Julia's slow reaction, at first, is of surprise without knowing what could be the correct response to Susy's request. Her first reaction is negative; she does not want to break with the "armonía estética del danzón" (aesthetic harmony of danzón) that could only be achieved through a heteronormative dancing routine. Traditionally, as Julia continues, the big body and strength of the man should lead in dancing, and, in opposition, the softness/passivity of the female body will follow and be the object of admiration and physical manipulation. By asking Julia to teach her to dance "as a woman," Susy is also asking her to trespass her own sense of womanhood and identity, inviting her to experience a different role, as a "man." In order to continue with the theatrical and apparent heteronormative dancing "harmony," Susy suggests to Julia: "Just remember how Carmelo used to hold you and hold me in the same way." With this statement, Susy confirms that gender is a performance (Butler 1990): when Julia finally accepts to perform the "masculine" role to teach Susy, as such, it is not completely unknown to her since she has been the spectator of masculinity in dancing since she was a child.

This pivotal moment triggers new ways of experiencing dancing, especially when Julia finally dares to subvert the specific rule of "avoiding the gaze of your dancing partner," by later looking directly into the eyes of a man she likes. This important transformation, becoming an agent by enjoying the power of gazing, is only possible after Susy expresses how much she enjoys dancing and playfully looking at her partner. Susy's pleasure for life and her courage to own her transgender identity helps Julia begin a negotiation between the traditional discourses on gender and a more democratic way to experience her sense of womanhood.

From Object to Subject: Julia's Gaze as an Expression of Desire and Agency

One of the most interesting aspects of *Danzón* is the playful tone used to subvert the patriarchal discourses and practices that limit the life of the protagonist. As someone who travels alone, she faces the potential punishment that society has imposed on women who dare to live without the protection of a man. At the beginning of Julia's trip to Veracruz, right after she exits the train station, the streets of the port are depicted as dominated by the presence of male individuals. This creates a sense of awkwardness for her. Once she meets Susy, however, who becomes her friend and accomplice, Julia visits several spaces that are still traditionally dominated by men, but she gains more confidence and transcends the position of being an object or ornament, becoming an agent with desires and a strong will, even within those confining spaces.

A sequence that clearly exemplifies Julia's transformation is situated right at the dock in Veracruz, which is full of ships and male sailors. Following Susy's recommendations, she wears a flowy red dress that perfectly denotes the actress' sculptural body. Once again, she is looking for Carmelo. As she walks on the dock contemplating the big ships, she also gets the attention of the male gaze. In that "masculine" space her presence seems to destabilize the operations of the day. At first, this sequence follows a traditional formula in which the body is objectified both by the camera and the eyes of the male figures in the frame. Even a crane, that clearly evokes a long phallus, seems to be interested in interpellating Julia while she roams the area to find Carmelo. Right after she sees, however, the Greek ship in which Carmelo might have been traveling, she continues walking about without knowing where to go. That moment of emptiness produces in her a profound transformation. Abandoning her search, at least for that moment, allows her to start to look at other objects, people, and, in general, her surroundings. It is probably the first time in many years that Julia allows herself to sightsee and people-watch without a specific purpose. The first objects she admires are the huge ships highlighting the use of humor and a nostalgic tone in María Novaro's films. The names of the ships evoke the watershed moment that the film represents in so many ways: Julia gets excited when she sees a ship named after one of her favorite danzón songs, "Lágrimas Negras" [Dark Tears]. The overlapping of illusion or nostalgia for the past, with the evident transformation of the character finally looking directly at other objects of interest, is crucial to understanding Novaro's filmic universe. The next ship she sees has the name "Puras Ilusiones" [Only Illusions], playfully evoking the romantic and very improbable dreams of Julia, who is hardly completing the illusion or fantasy of finding Carmelo in Veracruz.

Interestingly, the playful tone of this sequence is achieved through a swift use of the camera to represent Julia's gaze. From that perspective, the sequence becomes a moment of epiphany for the protagonist, who allows herself not only to timidly look at her surroundings but also at the figure of an attractive young man who suddenly appears on a boat's deck. At this moment, Julia's eyes become the focus of the close-up frame, from which the main character dares to express desire through her gaze by directly looking at the young man's body. She also plays with her hair and discovers that the name of the boat in which the young man works, "Me Ves y Sufres" [You look at me and you suffer], is a metaphor for her own position as a gazer, considering that her supposed suffering is pure enjoyment. The camera and the sequence denote a subversion to the traditional practices of gender and sexuality wherein now the female element is capturing the object of desire through her eyes, being also in charge of the romantic/sexual chase. By looking at the object of her attraction, Julia recovers, or even experiences for the first time, the ability to express her sexual desire. Her gaze, which in this sequence is depicted through several shots that travel back and forth between the gazing subject and the gazed object, defines not only what she sees but also the relationship with what she sees. Julia's gaze, as Lauro Zavala argues, is the site of Novaro's cinematic enunciation as a woman filmmaker, proposing through this sequence new cultural meaning. In this sense, the sequence establishes a "gazing system" [sistema de miradas] that will redefine the traditional male gaze (Laura Mulvey 1989), still present in most cinematic productions around the world. Thus, Novaro's cinema is truly innovative: on the one hand, she creates the power of enunciation to historically excluded identities such as Julia or Susy in the film—or in other words, as an intradiegetic enunciation. At the same time, *Danzón* establishes innovative extradiegetic dialogues by creating a female gaze in Mexican film production, powerfully feminizing, as Dolores Tierney argues, the very patriarchal symbolic Mexican culture and spaces (Tierney 364).

As in a game of coincidences, Julia and her object of desire, Rubén, bump into each other later in the film. In that encounter, she has doubts about looking at him directly, but, in the end, she dares to experience a short-lived affair, despite the age difference between them. With this sudden relationship, she pushes the limits of her identity that, up to that point, regulated her behavior in society: first, she abandons the asexuality historically required of virginal womanhood in Mexico; secondly, she truly enjoys her intense sexual encounters with Rubén without having the expectation of marriage or love. The affair is a temporary condition that has its own purpose, not to become the source of forever happiness in her life.

The enjoyment of Julia as a desiring woman is richly depicted in her last encounter with Rubén. After making love to him, preventing the spectator from witnessing the actual sexual encounter, Julia contemplates the body of her young lover. A sheet barely covers Rubén's bottom, allowing the spectator, who adopts Julia's point of view, to enjoy the naked body of the male character. One more time, Novaro uses the camera to become Julia's eyes. Wearing a femme fatale black nightgown, and smoking the traditional after-sex cigarette, the trajectory of her eyes goes from Rubén's head to his toes. It is worthwhile to mention that for this particular sequence, it was the director, María Novaro, who operated the camera to achieve this evocative yet sexually charged scene. The camera not only looks at Rubén but almost seems to caress his body. It is, indeed, a sensual and fluid use of the cinematic camera. This fluidity represents, in some way, Julia's new position as a woman. She is no longer regulated by the rigid rules of "danzón cerrado," but she is creating her own rules and movements. Dancing danzón will continue to be a source of enjoyment for her, but she will also be able to integrate other sources of pleasure into her life such as her sexual encounters.

Julia breaks with the social scripts that define women as passive elements in society. In addition, she goes beyond the binary construct of womanhood that has characterized Mexican culture. She does not have to behave as a virgin or as a fallen woman. In other words, enjoying her own sexuality will no longer be a reason for social punishment. As the owner of the hotel where Julia stays, confirms, "lo bailado nadie te lo quita" [no one can take from you that pleasure you already enjoyed] as she prepares herself to return to Mexico City. The new Julia returns to her daughter, to her work, and even to danzón. The final sequence, however, proposes a new attitude: one where she will establish her own rules such as looking into Carmelo's eyes when she finally dances with him. She is taking the initiative to express desire; she is in the end who decides the direction of her own life.

Bibliography

Mulvey, Laura. *Visual and Other Pleasures.* Houndmills, Basingstoke, Hampshire: Macmillan, 1989.
Novaro, María. Conferencia Magistral de María Novaro, 28 de junio de 2011. > http://www.casamerica.es/en/cine/conferencia-magistral-de-maria-novaro.
Sutherland, Romy. "María Novaro." *Senses of Cinema*, vol. 23, January 30, 2011. http://sensesofcinema.com/2002/greatdirectors/novaro/.
Tierney, Dolores. "Silver Sling-backs and Mexican Melodrama: Salón México and Danzón." *Screen*, vol. 38, no. 4, December 1997, pp. 360–371.
Zavala, Lauro. "Film Analysis and Contemporary Mexican Narrative: A Theoretical Approach to a Reflexive Point of View." > http://lanic.utexas.edu/project/etext/llilas/vrp/zavala.html.

CHAPTER 2

Brincando el Charco: Portrait of a Puerto Rican (Frances Negrón-Muntaner. 1994, U.S./Puerto Rico)

Abstract Frances Negrón-Muntaner's film is considered an experimental experience of queerness and national identity, while also intersecting it with racial discourses in the Puerto Rican national imaginary. *Brincando el Charco* deconstructs and reconstructs Puerto Rican identity by questioning its basic performance premise: the family. Each member has a specific gender role and the main character, Claudia, does not follow the one assigned to her. She is a lesbian and her definition of national identity is completely different from what is expected from her. Although the material may provide for a melodramatic perspective, Negrón-Muntaner breaks with this approach by focusing on reflections about her different experiences with Puerto Rican and other diverse communities in Philadelphia. The "history" represented in the film is fragmented, interrupted, and artificial as any other cultural production, but it has a conscience of artificiality that allows the spectator to trace a new kind of national identity, queering the national performance in a hopeful light for inclusion.

Keywords Puerto Rican identity • Lesbian • Family • National identity • Puerto Rican film • National cinema

Production

Production	Hipspic Productions, Women Make Movies, Independent Television Service, National Latino Communications Center, National Endowment for the Arts, Philadelphia Foundation, Temple University, ASTRAEA, National Lesbian Action Foundation (among others)
Direction	Frances Negrón-Muntaner
Cinematography	Jim Denault, Chris Emmanouilides
Producers	Frances Negrón-Muntaner, Chris Emmanouilides (Associate), Cate Wilson, John Tyson (Line)
Screenwriter	Frances Negrón-Muntaner
Editing	Valerie Keller

Cast

Claudia	Frances Negrón-Muntaner
Ana	Natalia Lazarus
Father	Oscar Colón
Mother	Miriam Cruz
Brother	Edgardo Porrata

Synopsis

Claudia Marín is a young Puerto Rican photographer living in Philadelphia. Struggling as an artist, she shares an apartment with her partner and successful lawyer, Ana. Claudia receives the news that her father died in Puerto Rico and she finds herself at a crossroads: to stay in Philadelphia and mourn her father from a distance, or to go back to the island and face her past, the memory of her father's homophobia and her family's distance. While considering what to do, the fictionalized world of Claudia and Ana is opened and cultural reflections regarding Puerto Rican identity, history, diaspora, language, and sexuality are presented. To face her father's ghost will be to face her heteropatriarchal nation, and Claudia needs to define her own identity before returning to Puerto Rico.

Director's Take: Frances Negrón-Muntaner (1966–)

Frances Negrón-Muntaner was born in Santurce, Puerto Rico. The daughter of academics, she lived in Long Island when she was eight years old, during the early 1970s. After completing her undergraduate studies at the University of Puerto Rico in Río Piedras, Negrón-Muntaner left the island in 1986. Her original plan was to continue her sociology studies, but she became a reporter, which shifted her views regarding the Puerto Rican diaspora and what it meant to live in the United States. As she affirmed in an interview with Jaditza A. Aguilar Castro, "For the first time, I experienced, in my own flesh and blood, living among the Puerto Rican communities that I only read about in urban sociology books" (*Cine y vídeo puertorriqueño*, 178, translation from Spanish). This realization was the beginning of her cinematographic view: a kind of in-between perspective as an academic and as a direct part of the diaspora community, which allowed her to reflect on her identity and her affiliations with Puerto Rico.

After five months in Philadelphia, Negrón-Muntaner went back to school and completed a Master's degree in film and anthropology at Temple University (1991, 1994) and a Ph.D. in Comparative Literature at Rutgers University (2000). Due to her work as a filmmaker, she had received fellowships from the Ford, Truman, Rockefeller, and Pew foundations, among others. Her cinematographic productions focus on a wide variation of topics, but all have in common an identity anxiety, the search for a place of belonging, either in history or in the community (Caribbean, Puerto Rican, or urban). She produced two other films: *AIDS in the Barrio* (1989) and *War in Guam* (2015), and published her academic work, such as the co-edited books *Puerto Rican Jam: Rethinking Colonialism and Nationalism* (1997), *None of the Above: Puerto Ricans in the Global Era* (2007), and her single-authored book *Boricua Pop: Puerto Ricans and the Latinization of American Culture* (2004).

Negrón-Muntaner's academic and film perspectives depart from the same concern: to destabilize the metanarrative of national discourses by applying a queer gaze or perspective. This queer approach is not limited to queer theory. By means of a queer gaze, she is able to disarm and deconstruct the performance around a cultural concept or political position in order to demonstrate its relative value in history, either in Puerto Rico or in the diaspora. The director starts to define her queer perspective as "another cinema," in which she attempts to conciliate her genuine concerns as a Puerto Rican and as a Puerto Rican academic, a difficult task, especially after the cold reception of her film *Brincando el Charco* in Puerto Rico. In "Beyond the Cinema of Other or Toward Another Cinema," published in *Aztlán* in 1999, Negrón-Muntaner explains the function of her films: "this kind of intervention is part of creating spaces where the challenge is not simply the representation of subaltern subjects, but of proposing other narrative modes for representing these subjects" (153).

Her proposal lies in a contingency of reconciliations that Gayatri Spivak questioned in her famous article "Can the Subaltern Speak?" (1988). Negrón-Muntaner offers an answer by offering cinema as a visual mediator that may find common ground between the director, owning the camera, and the subject in front of the camera. In commenting on this proposal on *Brincando el Charco*, she affirms: "I expected the film to answer the question of whether it is possible to return home, or at least to return to some houses in common. The answer is that, without doubt, it is possible to travel home through film, not as cinema of the other, but another cinema" (153). In her search for some "common houses" between the academic and the real world, the director and subject, Negrón-Muntaner prefers to gaze at the world through queerness in order to implode the metanarrative national discourses applied specifically in Puerto Rican cinema.

Negrón-Muntaner understands that national cinema is constructed around a performance, in which Puerto Rico's identity is determined by the application of traditional subjects: white, Catholic, heterosexual, and patriotic (patriotism defined as someone living on the island, in a constant fight with colonialist forces). By applying a queer look or gaze to this performance, Negrón-Muntaner deconstructs it. Nevertheless, this deconstruction is not accomplished by facing it with another absolute discourse (a.k.a nationalistic) but by piercing the national performance through fragmented voices and histories. In discussing *Brincando el Charco*, we can define the characteristics of Negrón-Muntaner's queer gaze.

COMMENTARY AND CONTEXT

The production of *Brincando el Charco: Portrait of a Puerto Rican*, though created in the diaspora, is settled as a counterargument to traditional Puerto Rican cinema. The island's cinema has its roots in the didactic vision of the División de Educación de la Comunidad [Division of Community Education] or DIVEDCO, the most influential film production company in Puerto Rico's history. DIVEDCO's films were used as a creative setting by many cinematographic artists during the 1950s and 1960s, such as Jack Delano (director and photographer) and Lorenzo Homar (poster designer and artist), but they had specific goals within the Department of Education. Such tasks were to inform the public about hygienic care, illiteracy, and Puerto Rican culture. Contemporary cinema still reflects this didactic ideology, for example, in Jacobo Morales' films such as *Lo que le pasó a Santiago* (1989) or *Linda Sara* (1994). The audience experiences the defense of Puerto Rican culture and identity. Negrón-Muntaner's efforts in her cinematic view fight to create a "ruptura política/ political rupture" against this nationalistic tendency: "This political rupture deals with my articulation of the nation, as well as my insistence on the autonomy and priority of other debates" (*Cine y video puertorriqueño,* 181, translation from Spanish).

Debating Puerto Rican national identity by integrating many and different discourses is the first characteristic of Negrón-Muntaner's queer gaze. The national discourse is the origin of the absolute performance the director breaks down in fragments: race, gender, sexuality, and class. *Brincando el Charco* starts with newsreel footage of the Puerto Rican Day parade in Philadelphia. A voice-over reflects on the main topics discussed in literature and the arts in Puerto Rico: Who are we? Where are we going? The island is a strong cultural nation, as Arlene Dávila defines in *Sponsored Identities* (1997), but it does not have political autonomy. This ambivalence is presented in the introduction of the film, but it does not only rely on documentary footage. It is also analyzed through the fictionalized character of Claudia Marín (Frances Negrón-Muntaner).

After the newsreel images, the camera follows Claudia as she is taking pictures of a male dancer/voguer in her studio and, later, developing them in her lab. While completing this task, we hear Claudia's voice-over asking questions about Puerto Rican identity and, after the camera stops to watch the dancer's picture, we hear *his* voice and watch his testimony not only as a Puerto Rican but as a gay man. By breaking the genres of fiction and documentary, mixing them both in a dance of images, voice-overs, and testimonies, Negrón-Muntaner achieves the goal of moving beyond the traditional cinematic view of exploring Puerto Rican history and identity. She lays out the conflict between the image and its significance, how the spectators interpret it, and what conclusions she or he can make regarding this ethnic and cultural identity.

Traditional cinema in Puerto Rico guides the spectators to assume a strong national identity, takes her or him by the hand, and depicts the traditional Puerto Rican characteristics of whiteness, heteronormativity, and anti-colonialism. *Brincando el Charco* distances itself from this perspective by rupturing this image and allowing the voice of the participants to take over. As Gilberto M. Blasini discussed in his review of the film "Hybridizing Puerto Ricanness" (2008):

The juxtaposition and its subsequent destabilization of the traditional definition of the cinematic modalities of the fiction film and the documentary become the avenue for re-reading and reconstructing Puerto Rican history in such a way that it incorporates traditionally marginalized sectors, both in the island and the U.S., such as migrants, blacks, and sexual minorities. (198)

Through the character of Claudia, Negrón-Muntaner reflects on her own questions and concerns. The use of newsreels allows for an analysis of the different events that integrate Puerto Rican identity. Nevertheless, it is with the testimonies of the different participants that a "polyphonic text" (Blasini 198) is created and a dialogue and possible solutions are given for a reconstruction and reconsideration of what it means to be Puerto Rican.

It is critical to understand that the film took five years to produce, roughly from 1989 to 1994. Throughout this time, celebrations of the quincentennial of Columbus' arrival to the Americas were starting to be planned; thus, discourses around postcolonial identity and historical reparations were strengthened in Latin America and the United States as a resistance to the effects of imperialism in the old colonies and the new stances on neoliberalism. While academia and the general public were attempting to sort out the various voices claiming a space in history, new approaches to how to write and read history began to develop. *Brincando el Charco* with its subtitle *Portrait of a Puerto Rican*, where its protagonist is not a traditional Puerto Rican, inscribes itself into this discussion of new historicism.

For many directors in Puerto Rico or in the United States, Claudia would not be the first choice to represent the island. Her gender, her sexuality, her world view, and her location undermine the traditional image of a Puerto Rican. By writing and choosing her, Negrón-Muntaner displays a second queer gaze characteristic: crisis as a road to reflection. Claudia is not a subject in crisis at the beginning of the story; she knows who she is and whom she loves. Her crisis begins when her father dies and she needs to make a decision to either go back to Puerto Rico to face her family or to stay and never resolve her loss. This crossroad opens the space to different discourses and intertwines Claudia's concerns with others. In the end, she is not the emblematic image or portrait of a Puerto Rican, but one of the many voices searching for a space both in the diaspora community and on the island.

Ambivalent, fragmented, polyphonic, and non-traditional identities are the main characteristics of Negrón-Muntaner's queer gaze. How to display such identities cinematically is a challenge that she managed to achieve by mixing fiction and documentary styles and techniques. These techniques are many and will fragment, interrupt and offer new histories in order to allow the spectators to decide what they think about Puerto Rico, national identity, and life in the diaspora.

Fragmenting History: Photographs and Testimonies

National histories and the search for national identities are always presented as a chronological and linear venture that creates a narrative with a complete sense of self and purpose. These constructions are internalized and, after many decades, they are still not questioned or problematized. In *Brincando el Charco*, Negrón-Muntaner breaks down the national constructions and internalizations to offer a fragmented—and more real—approach to the realities of Puerto Ricans in the diaspora and in connection with the island. This fragmentation of history is represented by cinematic techniques that are aware of the artificial narration the director is creating. It moves between the fictionalized world and real events and discussions around Puerto Rico's national identity.

Claudia, who is a photographer, is working on an exhibit based on different portraits of Puerto Ricans in the diaspora. After a short prologue, on which the main questions that will be discussed in the film are presented ("Who are we? What is our common destiny?"), we see Claudia on a photo shoot production. A male dancer/voguer is posing. While she is working on his pictures in the lab, the revealing, both literally and metaphorically, begins. A close-up shows the audience how the picture begins to appear on paper and a voice-over helps the spectators to hear and see who is behind the picture. The dancer/voguer explains who he is and from where he departed to find his destiny: "I do not choose to be gay. I mean, who wants to live a lifestyle where you are a minority within a minority? Because I'm Hispanic and I'm gay." This statement is inscribed in a bigger framework that Negrón-Muntaner is exploring: How to relate the discourses of colonialism, national identity, and sexuality? Like one of her characters asks: What does that (nationality) have to do with you as a lesbian? In order to answer these questions, Negrón-Muntaner does not speak only through Claudia and her photographic work but gives voice to the pictures. By allowing the participants to speak (with no names and no references until the credits), the spectators will be able to see and hear the different perspectives and versions of Puerto Rico's history and national identity. These perspectives range from sexuality issues, and race, to social class inequalities.

The topics of discussion are triggered by both the national constructs given to Puerto Ricans since birth and the diasporic experience. Just like the dancer/voguer explores the conflicts of a minority within a minority (being gay and Latino), a Black Puerto Rican student also presents the conflict of first impressions. Again, the spectators are presented with her testimony via the picture that Claudia took of her. The picture in itself complements what her testimony presents: the ambiguity of being Black and Puerto Rican. The image presents her beautifully sitting on a chair, looking down, as if refusing to see the image in the mirror behind her. Then, we hear and see her testimony in Spanish: "Estaba bien ingenua en términos de cuál era la experiencia aquí, histórica, en términos de los negros y de los blancos y los puertorriqueños ... están bien segregados el uno y del otro y ... hay unos estereotipos de parte de cada grupo hacia otro grupo [I was so naive in terms of what the historical experience is here in terms of Blacks and whites and Puerto Ricans ... they are very segregated from one another and ... there are some stereotypes from one group to the other]." After these candid expressions, a fictionalized scene of her at school is presented.

Two Black men are talking about relationships. One of the guys tells the other one how there are many beautiful Black women when the Black Puerto Rican student enters the scene to make a phone call. They notice how pretty she is and she becomes a possible flirting prospect for one of the guys. Then, she speaks Spanish, breaking down the first impression the men had of her as an African-American:

> Man 1: Alright, alright. I thought she was a sister.
> Black Puerto Rican student: What do you mean? I'm a sister.
> Man 2: What he means is that... (smiles) Well, where are you from?
> Black Puerto Rican student: (In testimony): Entonces a mí me preguntan de dónde yo soy, yo digo que soy de Puerto Rico. Entonces ahí es como que 'ah, ¡Puerto Rico! (smiling) ¡Yo nunca había visto una mujer tan negra de Puerto Rico!' [Then they ask me where I am from, and I say I am from Puerto Rico. Then that's when they go like 'ah, Puerto Rico! (smiling) I had never seen such a dark woman from Puerto Rico!'].

This scene, as many others throughout the film, is emblematic of how Negrón-Muntaner fragments national history and identity by playing with images, documentary, and fiction. African heritage is a discussion that is not openly considered in Puerto Rican films and is silenced in cultural or historical accounts. By placing the discussion outside the island's frontier, the director lets the audience know that it is not a topic that will naturally come from the island's citizens but one that arises and is developed when the citizens experience the diaspora and start to negotiate a new meaning to their identity.

Other negotiations with new identities and realities are cinematically performed in the same way as with the Black Puerto Rican student: a picture is presented and it complements the story that we will hear, we listen and see the participant's testimony, we go back to the fictionalized world, either by the same participant or through Claudia's thoughts, and then the spectators are moved on to another topic. In between these testimonial scenes, other performances take place, such as the historical accounts from a witness to the move of Puerto Ricans to Harlem (later known as El Barrio), the declamation of the poem "Purely Perfect Puerto Rican," or images from the first Puerto Rican Gay Pride Parade. Because of the direct relationship the pictures and the testimonies have with the fictional world of the main character, these other mixtures of performances serve as historical backgrounds on which national history and identity are fragmented.

The variety of faces and testimonies offer a more complex answer to the original questions, "Who are we? and what is our destiny?" presenting a diversified "we" and multiple destinies related to the in-betweenness of beliefs in the island and the diaspora. The complexity is arranged as a fragmented, but intertwined, history. Nevertheless, this is not the only technique the director creates for her counterargument. History needs not only to be fragmented to see its diversity. It also needs to be interrupted.

Interrupting History: Intertitles

The interruption of history is done by an old cinematic technique: the intertitles (or title cards). Often, the intertitles serve to divide the main story of the film into sections. These cards will narrate the argument chronologically, thematically, or by each character. They serve as signals to the spectators that, though the story is fragmented, it is still related. Negrón-Muntaner's use of intertitles, however, has more than one function. They serve as a break in the narration but also as a way to confront the spectators' expectations and to amplify their perspective.

The main argument, Claudia's resolve and her search for an identity before going back to the island, is divided into four sections, each signaled by an intertitle, "Uno," "Dos," "Tres," and "Pesca'o," titles that correspond to a children's game in Puerto Rico equivalent in the United States to the game "Statues." The first three sections invite the spectators to watch Claudia's process and train of thought in a progressive way. Nevertheless, the intertitles association with this children's game implies movement, though not in an organized manner. In the game, each child needs to move as fast as they can while the person in the front counts "Uno, dos, tres." When the person in the front says the word "Pesca'o," the children need to freeze, no matter where they are. The same implication is in Claudia's identity search. No matter where each subject moves in her or his search for an identity resolution, they need to move forward and beat the chances of staying frozen. The first three segments work around Claudia's personal search, but they also apply to other participants. In his review, Milton Ricardo Machuca offers an interpretation of this division: "In the opening segment, *Uno*, Claudia's world is explored ... *Dos*, probes history in order to understand national identity ... In *Tres*, Claudia views herself as a familiar stranger ... The final section, *Pesca'o*, considers the different strategies practiced by different Puerto Ricans to resolve their migratory dilemmas" (92–93). Though it is presented as a linear narrative, the implications of the game are juggled in this narration and a total solution is not offered. By using these intertitles, Negrón-Muntaner is guiding the spectator through the story, but also winking at another meaning into it, not clearly defined, and in constant movement.

The intertitles' guidance Machuca describes is interrupted when they serve as a means of confrontation with the spectator. While Claudia is trying to claim a new identity, she needs to face her sexuality and how it developed as part of her own national physical space. She fled Puerto Rico because her father was intolerant of her lesbianism. This patriarchal national figure haunted her. The disco was the magical place in which she was able to express herself, but by changing her physical space outside of the island and into the diaspora, she ended the enchantment. Until, one day, she explains, she saw how some men voguers claimed the dance hall: "Without knowing, they allowed me to imagine a space for the body that had no image." This body is hers, her own lesbian body, which through another picture/testimony, she presents as invisible: "La invisibilidad de las lesbianas tiene que ver, en general, con la invisibilidad de la sexualidad femenina ... ¿Qué van a hacer dos mujeres juntas en la cama? Eso es impensable, no hay un pene [The invisibility of lesbians has to do, in general, with the invisibility of female sexuality … What are two women going to do in bed together? That is unthinkable, there is no penis]." This testimony opens the film to a reflection of this physical lack of understanding of the female body in a sexual fantasy scene. It is in the presentation of these images that new intertitles confront the spectators in order to break down their beliefs. While women are on-screen kissing and caressing each other's bodies, the intertitles comment and ask questions: "What a lack … of imagination," "¿qué miras?/[What are you looking at]," "don't look," "do it." These words mixed up with the sexual images expand the shock the scenes may cause in the spectator. They are not describing what is being watched, but pushing a desire that for some may be prohibited because of heteronormative conventions. The sensuality of the bodies arouses fantasy; the words, controversy.

The interruption of history by the intertitles and their different function, as title guidance, confrontation, and amplification help to disarm the national metanarrative that is in question in the film. The intertitles are used to be provocative and reflective in order to face other perspectives of history and national identity that audiences usually do not find in traditional historical accounts. The interruptions are also a reminder of the artificiality of the film, a reminder of how other histories can also be artificial.

Negrón-Muntaner, by highlighting the artificiality of the narrative, is proposing a counterargument to understand the nation as multiple realities, ones that go beyond the limits of the island but also a return. Each of the characters presented in the film has "brincado el charco," "jumped the puddle," in one way or another, either coming out or going back, or negotiating a bridge between both spaces, but there are no solutions in the different alternatives. There is always a bend in the road that allows for new negotiations and reflections. Claudia found hers in her father's death and the various participants in confronting their own "minority inside the minority" issues, but such negotiations and reflections should not be considered absolute. The film claims a new space for Puerto Rican national history and identity, one that is a never-ending quest.

Bibliography

Aguilar Castro, Jaditza A. "Frances Negrón Muntaner (Entrevista)." *Cine y vídeo puertorriqueño 'Made in USA,'* Programa de Estudios de Honor UPR, 2000, pp. 177–183.

Blasini, Gilberto M. "Hybridizing Puerto Ricanness." *Caribbean Studies*, Vol. 36, No.1, June 2008, pp. 196–200.

Dávila, Arlene. *Sponsored Identities: Cultural Politics in Puerto Rico*, Temple U Press, 1997.

Negrón Muntaner, Frances. "Beyond the Cinema of the Other or toward Another Cinema." *Aztlán*. Vol. 24, nN.2, Fall 1999a, pp. 149–154.

Negrón Muntaner, Frances. "When I was a Puerto Rican Lesbian: Meditations on *Brincando el Charco: Portrait of a Puerto Rican*." GLQ, Vol. 5, No.4, 1999b, pp. 511–526.

Spivak, Gayatri. "Can the Subaltern Speak?" *The Post-Colonial Reader*, edited by Bill Ashcroft, Gareth Griffiths & Helen Tiffin, Routledge, 1995, pp. 24-28.

PART II

Anxieties and Sexualities

CHAPTER 3

Tan de Repente (Diego Lerman. 2002, Argentina)

Abstract An internationally co-produced film, Diego Lerman's opera prima, *Tan de Repente* (2002), is directly connected to the so-called New Argentine Film by portraying a gray image of Buenos Aires and its inhabitants. In addition to analyzing some of the main features in Lerman's oeuvre, the chapter centers on three moments in which the status quo and its corresponding inertia are shattered, presenting, both visually and discoursively, innovative approaches to the concept of relationships, love, desire, and the notion of happiness. The everyday life of a young working-class woman is disrupted through the actions of the other two protagonists: two young lesbians who live their lives on the margins of what is considered acceptable. This black-and-white film proves to have a complex repertoire of emotions that break with traditional conventions of representation, allowing the spectators to contemplate other ways of defining the female and lesbian identity in post 2000 crisis Argentina.

Keywords Lesbian • Lesbianism • Road movie • Class • Sexuality
• Argentinian cinema

© The Author(s), under exclusive license to Springer Nature
Switzerland AG 2024
D. Abreu-Torres et al., *Latinidad and Film*,
https://doi.org/10.1007/978-3-031-56118-4_3

Production

Production	Hubert Bals Fund, Lita Stantic Producciones, Nylon Cine
Director	Diego Lerman
Cinematography	Diego del Plano, Luciano Zito
Producers	Sebastian Ariel, Diego Lerman, Nicolas Martínez Zemborain, Lita Stantic
Script	Diego Lerman, María Meira, Eloisa Solaas
Film Editing	Alberto Ponce, Roli Rauwolf, Benjamin Ávila

Cast

Marcia	Tatiana Saphir
Mao	Carla Crespo
Lenin	Verónica Hassan
Blanca	Beatriz Thibaudin
Delia	María Merlino
Felipe	Marcos Ferrante

Synopsis

Marcia is a young woman living in Buenos Aires and working in a lingerie store. While living a very ordinary life between her job, anonymous calls to her ex-boyfriend, exercising, and commuting to her work, Marcia unexpectedly meets Mao and Lenin, two young women who are punks wandering the streets of Buenos Aires. Mao is fascinated by Marcia and wants to have sex with her. Threatening Marcia with a knife, Lenin helps Mao kidnap her. Both punks steal a taxi and take Marcia out of the city. At the end of this first part of the journey, Mao and Lenin have taken Marcia to the beach, a place she had never visited. Eventually, the three young women are stranded while returning to Buenos Aires and Mao and Lenin decide to go to Rosario. At first, Marcia is hesitant but then decides to follow them. Thus, a second journey starts for all of them, a potential voyage of self-discovery and empowerment.

Director's Take: Diego Lerman (1976–)

Diego Lerman is part of a group of independent directors that gained recognition after the economic downfall of Argentina in 2001. His work as a director has primarily dealt with strong female characters immersed in either family or political crises. These crises are a product of the country's financial struggles but also offer a different point of view on how to narrate the nation and how the country is transforming. According to Pablo Trapero, another independent director: "What we have in common [as directors] is that many things are excluded from our films, such as the notion of the omniscient discourse of a director who knows the truth and interprets and illuminates it for the spectator" (NYT). Denying that omniscient perspective is precisely the focus Lerman follows in his films: he prefers small stories, from quotidian life, which may be disrupted due to external events, but with characters that fight to continue being ordinary.

Lerman studied Sound and Design at the University of Buenos Aires, and Drama at the Municipal School of Dramatic Arts, which provided him with a particular view on how to direct his actors and what expectations to place on them: "he tried his luck as an actor and developed his abilities as a director–largely because he firmly believes that a director needs to understand what actors go through. 'I relate to my actors in a very intuitive way, with no particular method'" (Suárez 20). This relationship between small stories and an intimate relationship with his actors responds to a creative need to avoid big narratives and to directorially swim against influences such as the iconic film *La Historia Oficial* (1985). To this point, Lerman affirms: "I never set out to prove a thesis. The important thing is the writing process itself and not what I think about it, because what I think while writing is radically different from what I think during production, which, in turn, is totally different from what I think while editing" (Suárez 20). Thus, his approach to film as a director is fragmented and reactive to the conditions of the narrative itself, not necessarily having a big purpose. In *Tan de Repente*, for example, the storyline diverges from a thriller film to a road movie to a facts-of-life or family film. Considering these constant movements, it may be concluded that the film represents the need for the escapism many felt after Argentina's financial crisis of 2001. In its fragmented development, however, and focus on the small stories of each character, the escapism disappears and a more reflective version of the film takes over. The characters may move, but the narrative's only aim is to testify on the ordinary relationships: friendships, family, and lovers.

The point of view that Diego Lerman develops became a fresh new start for Argentinian cinema. As a boy, Lerman experienced the dictatorial persecution of his family, as his father was a labor leader in hiding (NYT). To some extent, his films are also a game of "hide and seek," as his ordinary stories still are embedded in Argentina's crisis and histories. Nevertheless, it is the small things, the small gestures, that matter in his filmographic world. As Jamie Russell affirms in his review of *Tan de Repente*: "By celebrating the importance of our relationships with others, it warns of the necessity of appreciating each moment before the cruel suddenness of life takes its toll" (Russell n.p.). It is in the appreciation of the small stories that Lerman finds his voice and his push to also create strong female characters who fight for their own ordinary stories.

Commentary and Context

Tan de Repente as a feature film was born from a short film titled *La Prueba* (1998), inspired by a novel, as many of Lerman's features, in this case one by César Aira. Working with the same actresses in *Tan de Repente*, the short film won the 2000 Buenos Aires International Festival of Independent Cinema (BAFICI) competition, which allowed Lerman time to write the feature film script by getting a scholarship at the San Antonio de los Baños Film School in Cuba (Suárez 20). *La Prueba*'s story starts with the meeting of Mao, Lenin, and Marcia in Buenos Aires and ends with their road trip to the beach. The beach scene, in which Mao and Lenin present to Marcia the sea, is the last scene. *Tan de Repente* allows us to observe what happens afterward in the story of these three young women and where their travels take them (Fig. 3.1).

Before delving deep into the analysis, it is necessary to address the genres and narratives of the film, which does not allow for a clear classification. Most reviewers, however, agree it is a road movie. Traditionally, a road movie is a journey of self-discovery led by a literal journey from point A to B: "The road in the road movie is never just a background: it is

Fig. 3.1 Marcia receives an offer from Mao and Lenin

typically both the motivation for the narrative to happen and also the place that allows things to occur. Instead of being just a transitional space between A and B, it is this space itself between A and B that becomes the focus of the road movie" (Archer 3). Thus, the road becomes a space in which personal crises are resolved, identities evolve, and relationships start or end.

As a genre, the road movie is fundamentally developed in the United States, as an "American" style. In the global cinematic space, however, the road movie plays alongside, or contrary to, this style in order to show "what happens when particular people at a particular time achieve the means of representing themselves on screen," and "a way of narrating ideas of identity and place, and as a vehicle for exploring our past, our troubled present, and even our uncertain future" (Archer 8). *Tan de Repente* plays with these characteristics of the road movie but also expands it by transmuting genres: from thriller to road movie to family movie. It is a transmutation because each genre represented is also in movement: walking, driving, hitchhiking, rowing, and each action is a constant movement with which the director highlights the fluidity of its characters and how each one will engage with the other(s). The thriller captivates the audience, uncertain of what may happen; the road movie provides a blueprint of a potential journey with which the spectators are better familiarized, and the facts-of-life of the family movie after getting to Rosario create an ambiance of reflection and wonder that avoids providing a clear ending.

The transmutation from thriller to road movie and to family movie also provides the space to create what in narratology is called a "weak narrative." According to Brian McHale, postmodernist poetry negotiates between two approaches to narration: the classical narrative in epic poetry in which a metanarrative moves the lyrics along the semantics of the reader, and modernist poetry, which completely denies the metanarratives. Dealing with the in-betweenness, postmodernist poetry still wants to narrate a story, especially individual stories, but it agrees with modernists that it cannot be manipulated by big narratives. Thus, representation of the story is created via fragmentation and interruption, the suspense of time, and plural storytelling: "Weak narrativity involves, precisely, telling stories 'poorly,' distractedly, with much irrelevance and indeterminacy, in such a way as to evoke narrative coherence while at the same time withholding commitment to it and undermining confidence in it" (McHale 165). While the metanarrative tells the reader what to pay attention to, the weak narrative allows the reader—and in film, the spectators—to fill in the gaps, participate actively in the storytelling, and bring its own conclusions. In *Tan de Repente*, Diego Lerman interrupts the fast pace and suspense of the thriller with the more languishing style of the road movie and, in the end, recreates a facts-of-life narrative that replaces all development with observation and reflection. As a weak narrative, flexible and fluid, the spectators are able to evolve with the characters and allow for the expected development, but not necessarily expecting a clear conclusion. By fragmenting the genres' narratives, Lerman is also providing an alternative path to narrating Argentine stories and how to represent and see its multiple characters.

This alternative of representation is reflected in the characterization of the film's protagonists. Before and during the kidnapping, Mao and Lenin were hard to read. As punks, they are living freely, taking what others have, not defining it as a robbery but as a necessity of life outside of social expectations. As spectators, we can see them stealing a motorcycle and playing in an arcade. On the other hand, Marcia is an open book. We can see her awkwardness in the city while she is walking fast and not looking at anybody, her out-of-place body in the lingerie store where she works, and her emotional standstill when calling her ex-boyfriend. She is not as free as Mao and Lenin, but she is subjected to her position as a worker and non-native of Buenos Aires. The gap in the bodily expression these characters portray may be traced back to class differences. Rosalind Galt affirms:

> Marcia is coded from the beginning as excessively corporeal … Her body is repeatedly foregrounded but always desexualized … Her distance from conventional patriarchal ideals of female beauty might tempt us to see Marcia as a social outsider, but she is also closely associated with labour. We first encounter her opening up the lingerie store where she works, keeping capitalist time as she works productively and responsibly. (75)

Although she is living in the city, which may imply more opportunities, Marcia needs to stick to her routine in order to not only live in the city but survive it. Mao and Lenin, on the contrary, "do not work, and instead are associated with crime and mobility … Their bodies are slim, dark and sleek, they have boyish cropped hair, wear stylish clothes, and exude confidence. Their outlaw bodies move fast, talk sexually, persuade and threaten. They live outside the symbolic strictures of the law and the capitalist economy" (Galt 76). Although we never know for sure why Mao and Lenin are wandering the streets and to which families they belong, in a crucial conversation before they kidnap Marcia, they interact with an employee in a Burger King. After the employee asks Lenin to throw away her cigarette, a tense exchange happens, but Lenin complies. Mao and Lenin start fantasizing about how to punish the employee and Marcia defends her:

> Mao: ¿Sabes cuál es la primera regla de estos lugares? [Do you know what the first rule of these places is?]
> Marcia: Sí. Calidad, servicio y… [Yes, quality, service, and…]
> Mao: No. El cliente siempre tiene la razón. Ahora bien, nosotras no somos clientes porque no consumimos nada. Pero si fuésemos a la caja, y compramos cualquier cosa, lo más barato de todo, nos ganamos la razón automáticamente. Bastante fácil, ¿no te parece? [No. The client is always right. Now, we are not clients because we're not consuming anything. But if we went to the register and buy anything, the cheapest item, we are automatically right. Really easy, don't you think?]
> Marcia: (Hesitant) Sí, qué sé yo, no tiene nada que ver. Mirá si le armás un escándalo y la chica que vino amablemente, encima pierde el trabajo. ¿Vos trabajaste alguna vez? [Yes, whatever. Look, what if you are disruptive and the poor girl who treated us nicely loses her job on top of everything? Have you ever held a job?]
> Mao: (Ticked off) ¿Qué tiene que ver? [What does that have to do with anything?]
> Marcia (Half smiling and affirmed): Se nota. [It shows].

While Mao is trying to make a philosophical argument against the labor market and its ties to capitalism and the strain on the body, Marcia is more practical and understands the consequences of not having access to capitalist goods and expectations. She, contrary to Mao, knows what labor is and how her body must fit in its structure in order to survive. Mao has not experienced this and, as a result, does not appreciate the constraints capitalism enforces on some experiences. Thus, this conversation allows for the spectators to better understand each character's background and point of view while creating a conflict between capitalist freedom and oppression.

The tension of the conflict exposed in the Burger King conversation represents what Galt has called "default cinema": defined as "a threat, a refusal to play by the rules of the game that carries a cultural charge as much as an economic one … [D]efault cinema is a form of filmmaking that thwarts neoliberal narratives, that defaults on the coerced promises of capitalist form and value" (63). By defaulting on traditional discourses of the cinematic genre, *Tan de Repente* not only fragments the narrative, but it also fragments the way in which the characters relate to capitalist origins. Furthermore, it relates to the idea of the "weak narrative," as it provides an anchor for the spectators to understand the characters, while at the same time confusing them by changing the narrative genre from a thriller to a road movie. Mao desires Marcia, and after their conversation, Marcia questions Mao's point of view. Mao then decides to prove her love by taking her to see the beach. An expected change is about to happen and the journey is just beginning.

The Journey of Mobilization

Two moments define the film's journey through different genres: the fragmented passage to Rosario and the familial solidarity that develops as soon as they arrive there. These two moments are key to Marcia's clear transformation and Mao and Lenin's self-discovery. After the cab they stole to go to the beach runs out of gas, the young women decide to walk. Marcia did not want to be left alone and followed Mao and Lenin. They hitchhike with a woman going to San Clemente. The ambiance in the car, for the spectators, is tense. We do not know what Mao and Lenin will do, if they will steal the car, and maybe hurt the woman, but in the end, nothing bad happens. They listened to her story about registering two orcas and they exited the car when the woman left them on the side of the road, near a diner. In this transitional move from the thriller to the road movie, the spectators are confused, but, just like Marcia, they begin to relax.

At the diner, Mao negotiates a second hitchhike to get to Rosario by offering a truck driver for Lenin to perform a sexual favor for him without Lenin's consent and when he tries to make a move, she resists. At the same time, the driver makes a sudden stop. A skydiver is in the middle of the road; apparently, a parachute malfunction provoked an accident. Marcia goes to check and the man dies in her arms. Although this is a surreal scene that may appear as an eccentricity from the scriptwriter, it serves as a symbolic reflection of the journey Marcia is taking: it feels like an adventure—she is willingly going to Rosario with Mao and Lenin, she is a proactive participant on the road trip—but this is an adventure that may end fatally. A transformation is foreshadowed, still reminiscent of the thriller movie.

This road trip to Rosario highlights the fragmentation of the characters' personal journey. It demonstrates Mao's selfishness, Lenin's go-with-the-flow resistance, and Marcia's reservations. It also breaks with the paradigms of the road trip film as point B is a fluid goal, one that arises because of the circumstances and not because there is a place they need/want to reach. Mao's intentions of keeping Marcia away from Buenos Aires is the only motivation that may be triggering the need to arrive at a destination, but this is not clearly stated nor manifested. Mao and Lenin's first thrilling and rash intentions when kidnapping Marcia are disregarded when they get to the sea, and Marcia is just a collateral participant in that first thrill.

When they finally reach Rosario, the entire ambiance of the film changes. They finally made it to point B, but the journey had not stopped. Meeting Blanca, Lenin's great-aunt, we learn that Lenin's name is Verónica and Mao finally gets her wish to have sex with Marcia. Staying in the same room with Mao, Marcia decides that she will have sex with her. Throughout the journey, she cooperated and felt a connection to Mao. They have sex and the tension that began the film, Mao's desire for Marcia, is fulfilled. The release does not announce a new climax, however. On the contrary, Mao, now wearing Marcia's clothing, goes to the kitchen and starts flirting with a young tenant in Blanca's house, Felipe, who has voyeuristically watched the young women having sex.

The fluidity of these scenes between sex and denial of any romantic connection breaks the expectations that have been forged since Mao saw Marcia. As a default cinema that breaks with cinematic expectations, it also breaks with queer romance by proposing a new kind of queering: Mao affirmed, at the beginning of the film, that she is not a lesbian, and although her performance with Lenin may reimagine her as lesbian, their actions never confirmed this assumption. Due to how lesbianism is treated in the film, Nayibe Bermudez Barrios concludes in her article that "in different degrees, by seeking to attenuate or negate lesbianism, the director and the cast of the film tried to control interpretation and, as can be inferred from the anxiety expressed, struggled to direct the film towards a heterosexual public" (23). By Mao wearing Marcia's clothing and flirting with Felipe, later taking him to a place he has never seen—just like she did with Marcia—she is establishing a more fluid sexual identity, one in which there is not only one or another way to express sexuality but several ways. By creating a queer space that is not settled, the film "refuses the mode of political representation that, under the rubric of world cinema, has all too often been co-opted into the cultural institutions of neoliberal globalization" (Galt 81). Just like capitalism has been questioned and complicated, queer subjects are also conflicted and do not rely on just one definition, but multiple ones, once again relying on the spectators to make sense of the narrative presented.

A New Kind of Domesticity

While Mao and Marcia's initial relationship starts to be redefined, Lenin/Verónica is reacquainting herself with her great-aunt Blanca. In gestures, taste, and subtle motions, a kinship is visually constructed, as if the director was trying to tell the spectators that in the future, Lenin may become Blanca, a foreshadowing that deconstructs Lenin's character. A selfish tomboy, navigating the streets of Buenos Aires, Lenin's representation was the opposite of domesticity. Her kinship with Blanca, however, changes her perspective and is not refused by Lenin/Verónica. In the daily routine of, chores and small-town dealings, her rough exterior presented while in Buenos Aires softens, creating an ambiance that moves beyond the thrills of the thriller movie and the discoveries of the road movie: it opens a new kind of identity by displacing the punk body and replacing it with a young woman reaching out for connections, for a family.

Marcia must deal with constructing and accepting her new identity. Now that she has explored a new way of connecting with another woman, Mao leaves her naked, literally and figuratively, that is, emotionally. Humiliated because she cannot wear Mao's clothing, she furiously tears up Mao's shirt and skirt, a symbolic action that moves her to a new journey: she is breaking with Mao's perspective of her. Wandering in the living room wrapped in a blanket, Delia, another of Blanca's tenants, invites her to her room so they can find some clothing. There, Marcia discovers Delia's artistry. A painter, Delia survives by teaching and, sometimes by selling, her work. As an artist, Delia lives in the interstices of capitalism, distanced from the urban landscape, on the margins, but still negotiating dominant society as she needs to consume to survive. Marcia looks at Delia's art with fascination, another way of life she discovers in this adventure. Delia provides her with a peasant's dress, a wink to the spectators that reminds us of another piece of the Burger King's conversation in which Mao mentioned that she could tell that Marcia was from "un pueblo," a small town because of her wardrobe. Marcia felt offended by this comment as she had been living in Buenos Aires for six years, but now here she was, in a peasant's dress that she liked. Marcia's body, identified by her labor and outside of beauty standards, is now reinvented and, to some extent, tamed by going back to her identity as a child from the margins of Buenos Aires, a peasant.

All three women, with the help of Blanca and her tenants, are transformed by domesticity and familial encounters: Mao goes out with Felipe to have ice cream; Lenin visits Blanca's old friends and helps her with chores; Marcia creates a new friendship and opens up about her own relationship struggles with Lenin. In the quietness of the provincial environment and the calmness of the house, all are transformed and redefined. In a scene at the end of the film, all the characters go out to town to visit the river, row together, and spend the day as a family. The tranquility of this scene completely contrasts with the chaos in which the film started and the tension is completely released. There is no explanation, no strong narrative that details these interactions, it is merely a family day. At the end of the film, the family simultaneously strengthens and changes after the death of Blanca. Mourning her aunt, Lenin/Verónica tries to reconnect with her mother and becomes Marcia's friend, chatting with her on the bus when returning to Buenos Aires; Mao takes Felipe to see the orcas; and Delia is tending to Blanca's house. Although separated, they all are still connected by the relationship they created around Blanca's house and its calmness. The film ends as a family movie, without a clear ending, but satisfied with the journey that brought three different and independent women together and in solidarity with strangers along the way.

Bibliography

Archer, Neil. *The Road Movie*. Columbia U Press, 2016. *JSTOR*, https://doi.org/10.7312/arch17647.

Bermúdez Barrios, Nayibe. "The Road Movie, Space, and the Politics of Lesbian Representation in Diego Lerman's *Tan de Repente*." *Revista Canadiense de Estudios Hispánicos*, vol. 35, no. 1, Otoño 2010, pp. 11–29. *JSTOR*, https://www.jstor.org/stable/23055665.

Galt, Rosalind. "Default Cinema: Querying Economic Crisis in Argentina and Beyond." *Screen* vol. 54, no. 1, Spring 2013, pp. 62–81. doi:https://doi.org/10.1093/screen/hjs068.

McHale, Brian. "The Case of Avant-Garde Narrative Poetry." *Narrative*, Vol. 9, No. 2, May 2001, pp. 161–167. *JSTOR*, https://www.jstor.org/stable/20107242.

Rohter, Larry. "Argentine Filmmakers' 'Smaller Focus'." *The New York Times*, 3 May 2005, https://www.nytimes.com/2005/05/03/arts/argentine-filmmakers-smaller-focus.html.

Russell, Jamie. "*Suddenly* (Tan de Repente) (2004)." *Movies, BBC*, 4 February 2004, http://www.bbc.co.uk/films/2004/02/04/suddenly_2004_review.shtml.

Suárez, Pablo. "A Road Movie With A Difference: *Suddenly* Announces The Arrival of a New Argentine Breakthrough." *FilmComment*, vol. 39, no. 5, 2003, pp. 20–21. *JSTOR*, https://www-jstor-org.trinity.idm.oclc.org/stable/43456616.

Tan de Repente [*Suddenly*]. Directed by Diego Lerman, Hubert Bals Fund/ Lita Stantic Producciones/ Nylon Cine, 2002.

CHAPTER 4

Madeinusa (Claudia Llosa. 2006, Perú)

Abstract As a powerful but controversial film, *Madeinusa* is a portrayal of an Indigenous community that questions the interactions of power and gender. The chapter analyzes how Llosa constructs a strong female character in a dystopian circumstance that dialogues with the Indigenous community's realities from which it is inspired. Corruption, sexual abuse, and sexual freedom are some of the themes exposed in the film and in which Madeinusa, the protagonist, thrives, as she is able to manipulate the desires of others to fulfill her own. The focus on the religious environment in which the storyline is developed emphasizes the breaking of the conventional rules of modesty and conservatism by imagining a god that turns his back on his children so they can play in absolute freedom as they break all social and familial contracts. Freedom, then, is what is desired by Madeinusa and what she pursues without regrets.

Keywords Desire • Self-discovery • Family • Sexuality • Sexual freedom • Religion • Peruvian cinema

Production

Production	Oberón Cinematográfica, Vela Producciones, Wanda Visión S.A.
Direction	Claudia Llosa
Cinematography	Raúl Pérez Ureta
Producers	Antonio Chavarrías
Screenwriter	Claudia Llosa
Editing	Ernest Blasi

Cast

Madeinusa	Magali Soler
Salvador	Carlos J. De la Torre
Chale	Yiliana Chong
Cayo	Juan Ubaldo Huaman
El Mudo	Kike Ortiz

Synopsis

For a number of days, in a rural town of Peru, there is a belief that God is temporarily "dead" and he is unable to see the sins of the inhabitants of that village. Madeinusa, a young woman, is selected to play the Virgin Mary during the "Tiempo Santo" or "Holy Time." At the same time, she meets Salvador, a character who will play a significant role in Madeinusa's decisions and future.

Director: Claudia Llosa (1976–)

Claudia Llosa was born in Lima, Perú, into a wealthy family. She studied communication studies at the Universidad de Lima and attended the Escuela Universitaria de Artes or Transforming Arts Institute (TAI) in Madrid where she gained experience in filming. She moved to Barcelona, where she started writing the script for *Madeinusa*. Her debut in filmmaking was with this film that presents the story of a young Quechua woman living in a religious, remote Peruvian town. *Madeinusa* premiered at the Sundance Film Festival in 2006, where it was nominated for the Grand Jury Prize. At the Havana Film Festival, it won for the best-unpublished script and was subsequently highly acclaimed at various other festivals. In 2009 Claudia Llosa released her second film *La Teta Asustada* (*The Milk of Sorrow*), which deals with the era of terrorism in Peru, from 1980 to

1992. Like *Madeinusa*, this film was acclaimed internationally, but it was less popular among Peruvian audiences. In 2010, *La Teta Asustada* was nominated for an Oscar in the Best Foreign Film Category. In 2012, she was the director of the short film *Loxoro*, produced by the Oscar winner Juan Carlos Campanella. This short won the Teddy Award at the Berlin International Film Festival. Her subsequent film, *Aloft* (2014), did not receive much attention from the critics. In the summer of 2021, she premiered her last film, *Fever Dream* (2021), at the San Sebastián International Film Festival in Spain.

Commentary and Context

Madeinusa is one of the most critically acclaimed and most controversial films in Peruvian cinematography. The motion picture has been appraised internationally, winning many prizes such as the prestigious Fédération Internationale de la Presse Cinématographique or the International Federation of Film Critics (FIPRESCI) Award in 2006. Most of the debate about this film began with the intervention from the Peruvian media that criticized what is considered the racist portrayal of the Indigenous community represented in Llosa's film (Palaversich 490). Nonetheless, *Madeinusa* creates a narrative with an uncommon portrayal of women having agency, and, at the same time, the breaking of the traditional and anthropological notion of associating women with nature and the landscape (Ortner 1997), especially Indigenous women like the film's protagonist. Acclaimed for the imaginary depiction of a religious festival in Peru, having a cast of almost 100% Indigenous actors, several critics asserted that it portrayed Indigenous people as naïve. In that sense, the film is believed to contribute to the stereotypes that have been associated with the Indigenous communities of Peru, especially like a group of people who live in an a-historic time. According to Bedoya and Velazquez, Llosa creates this town and story based on her own rules of verisimilitude; therefore, it is pure fiction. At the same time, she is not afraid to highlight serious problems such as incest and alcoholism that actually happen in Indigenous and non-Indigenous communities around the world.

In the story, we can see that the protagonist's father is consistently molesting his daughters during the "Tiempo Santo," an action which is accepted, and even encouraged, by the community. In the beginning, the spectators witness several dialogues between Madeinusa and her father, who pressures her to have sex with him even before the "Tiempo Santo." Peruvian critics highlight how it falsely represented the Andes and how to be "acclaimed internationally" means foreigners have a negative image of

Peru presented to them. Most of the criticism that Llosa received was from the Peruvian elite and not from Indigenous organizations. This gesture enables us to understand the lack of voice of the Indigenous groups in Peru in comparison to the Peruvian intelligentsia. Another critique is the fact that Llosa did not grow up in the village; rather, she comes from a family that is financially well-connected in Peru and beyond. Llosa is, in some way, seen as a foreigner trying to capture the life of Indigenous people according to her privileged point of view. Magaly Solier, the protagonist and Indigenous actress, was one of the strongest defenders of Llosa's work. She saw the film in a more positive light because it was a way of addressing the sexual abuse and other topics she witnessed but that were not addressed in her community.

Religion is another theme that plays a significant role in the film. It is what causes young Madeinusa to take a leap toward obtaining her freedom from her repressive community and her abusive father. The entire village is in "Tiempo Santo" when it is believed that God cannot see their sins, especially incest and other types of abuse that people are committing within their own families. This "Holy Time" and the certainty that her father wants to have sex with her, makes Madeinusa want to lose her virginity to Salvador, a foreigner, instead of her father, in order to gain control of her own body. Throughout the entire film, there is a relationship between the sacred and the profane given the importance of religion to the entire village; at the same time, once it is Holy Time the profane begins to unravel. This disorderliness is demonstrated through the various actions that occur during this time: from stealing a pig to having different lovers, even women who are generally oppressed participate in the ritual in different ways. Although the film focuses on Madeinusa interacting in several situations, she experiences double the oppression for being Indigenous and a woman. Through the eyes of Salvador, a white young, professional man from Lima, the spectators witness the hegemonic perspective that the director is criticizing. Despite the fact that Madeinusa is portrayed as an intelligent young woman, she is nevertheless depicted from a perspective that identifies her, and the other people of the town, outside history. In fact, "Tiempo Santo" is precisely a time in which God would be sleeping, not keeping a record of the human actions and sins that oppress the protagonist and other women and girls in her town.

In the end, Madeinusa escapes the town by herself, reclaiming her agency and her life. This young protagonist breaks barriers to achieve her goal of traveling to Lima to find her mother. By empowering an Indigenous woman with agency over her body and herself, this film is innovative and it opens new discursive spaces for Indigenous women. Her acts of escaping demonstrate her defiance of the heteropatriarchal order and how she is a catalyst of change, capable of leaving the town and the cultural customs that oppress her. Through *Madeinusa*, despite its various contradictions, Llosa undermines the conventional belief of a woman being tied to the land, to her home, and oppressive cultural tradition (Palaversich 497–498). Although moving away from her town should be recognized as the character's regaining her agency, inhabiting a big city like Lima (or Mexico City) is not ideal because Indigenous women suffer much discrimination and mistreatment from communities in these spaces as well. This film, therefore, should be considered an important watershed moment in Peruvian cinema that denounces the sociocultural abuse of women and girls, but in the end, it comes from a privileged perspective that does not consider the entire picture.

It's Holy Time!

Holy Time has finally started and all the villagers are excited and celebrating. At the beginning of the celebration Madeinusa meets Salvador, a white geologist from Lima, and a mutual attraction develops between them. The first time Salvador sees Madeinusa she is wearing a dress as if she were representing the Virgin during Holy Time. He is interested in the festival and, at the same time, feels like a foreigner in his own country. Madeinusa is wearing the costume that will be used once the festival begins. The moment when he sees her for the first time is beautiful and poetic. On the other hand, Madeinusa feels this attraction to Salvador since he is the epitome of what she has seen in the media from the "exterior world": he is not only white, he has mannerisms from Lima, and, therefore, he is considered a global citizen. For example: he wears very comfortable clothes such as what one wears when going camping; he also has a more informal approach to others, demonstrating his privileged social capital. After a couple of encounters through the town, the two of them finally meet in "Tiempo Santo." In one particular scene, when the entire town is celebrating "a lo grande [in a big way]" with music, dancing, drinking, and breaking social norms, Madeinusa decides to have sex with Salvador. This decision is daring because the tradition of the town states that the father of the young woman will take her "virginity." Madeinusa takes control over her own body, breaking the heteropatriarchal system from being an icon of immobility, like the Virgin, to taking charge of her life. She liberates herself from the gender norms and decides exactly what will happen during that night.

In terms of camera work, this sequence is dominated by medium shots displaying the actions and emotions that Madeinusa and Salvador express. The lighting is used strategically throughout the scene. She is depicted with a candle illuminating her face. In the first glimpse, the innocent halo around her face reflects the purity of her Virgin Mary costume. Immediately the shot changes to a deep focus shot of Salvador secretly watching her from afar. He is not well lit so as to highlight how he is lurking in the shadows for he just escaped, with the help of Madeinusa, from a room where her dad, Cayo, had locked him in. Another medium shot of them reveals when she is taking Salvador with her; at this point his lighting changes from having half of his face lit to all of it as he follows her like he was in a trance or allured by her. The setting is also another important aspect because it creates the mood and gives reasoning about the character's actions. The scene where Madeinusa decides to have sex for the first time is in a private but also public space, by the wall of a house that is hidden from other people's view. The fact that the sexual act occurs by this wall exposes how a house is a "lived space that embraces mobility" (Holmes 211). The house is not only a place where women have to cook, clean, and be caretakers; at the same time, it is a reminder of the affective and oppressive dynamics that affect children and youngsters, as well as women, because there is a belief that what happens in the house is a private matter. In this sense, the place where they are having sex is on the "border" and it is certainly political: it is a house but it is also the street. In other words, she is breaking the limits of her own (domestic) identity. For the sexual encounter, Madeinusa has control over the whole situation; she guides Salvador to that corner and she lowers her underwear to have intercourse with him. Losing her virginity to someone else rather than to her father shows her act of defiance and vengeance for she now is aware that she has the right to do with her body as she pleases. She has deviated from her role of "nurturer" and "life giver" to one of an "agent of change" (Palaversich 498). In this sense, she has reversed the role of being a nurturer by "nature" (Ortner) and instead, she becomes a cultural catalyst of social change.

Madeinusa's name is another significant aspect of this scene sequence. Right after they have sex, she sees that Salvador's shirt has the words that, together, spell her name and she asks him why that is the case. He responds that "Made in USA" is not a real name and that she should have been named Rosa or María. Madeinusa states that she loves her name and that it belongs to her. Her last remark continues to emphasize the power she has because she does not allow Salvador's comments to make her feel embarrassed. Madeinusa's name alludes to her love of foreign places and also foreshadows her departure from her village. Another perspective of her name was as a metonym for the film. In Lima, her name carries the significance of the English language, but in Madeinusa's isolated village the meaning is not cared for; rather, it is the sound and the aesthetic feel of it. Her name highlights the ignorance of the town but also the freedom the village has from the globalized world (Holmes 211). Madeinusa begins to reclaim her agency through the beginning of Holy Time. She selects her first sexual partner, thereby rebelling against her town's heteropatriarchal rules. This protagonist is one step closer to breaking away from the norms to live the life she chooses even though she will have to overcome other obstacles that will allow her to be "free" while living in the country's capital of Lima where she will also encounter other types of discrimination for being an Indigenous woman.

The Attic with "Valuable" Objects

At one point, Cayo, Madeinusa's father, is drunk and talking to Salvador, the foreigner, about his impending departure. Cayo takes him to the attic where there are many trinkets that were offered to the Virgin and, among them as if she were one more "valuable object," is Madeinusa who is captive. It is important to state that the subversion she makes of the rules, having sex for the first time with Salvador instead of her father, elicits this "punishment" of being kept captive as well as being raped by her father just before going to the attic. We, as spectators, however, do not see this painful scene and instead, we learn of it from the perspective of her sister. The rape scene occurs so quickly, that some spectators can be confused, or in denial, about what is actually happening in the story.

Cayo picks a statue to offer as a gift, but Salvador declines the statue and breaks it. Cayo concludes that Salvador is going to leave empty-handed while Madeinusa is immobile in the background. This scene perfectly demonstrates the limitations women have due to the heteropatriarchal system that often considers them ornamental objects. In this case, after the father rapes her, she is not considered as "valuable" as before; therefore, she is on the verge of being "disposable."

The scene begins with a medium shot of the attic with all the gifts the town has offered to the Virgin. As the camera pans following both men, it then showcases all the different gifts. The dialogue is significant as it highlights the power Cayo has as the town's mayor and as a man as well. He states how he stores all those statues there to make the town believe that the Virgin has taken them all. He helps the Virgin by increasing the faith of the town and believes that the Virgin will repay him. The camera subtly continues to move to reveal Madeinusa sitting stagnantly in a corner. Just as she is exposed, Cayo tells Salvador emphatically to choose any of the objects in the room. This medium shot that first exposes her has a deep focus demonstrating the depth of her prison and how, even there, she has a limited space for there are many other statues that accompany her. Her face is not well lit, symbolizing her limited role as a woman. Even during the festive season of Holy Time, where there is no sin and no punishment, she is locked up in the attic for having sex. Her father categorizing her as a worthless thing dehumanizes her further as if she were a "disposable object."

As Cayo and Salvador continue talking, we see close-up shots changing between their faces. Cayo is stubbornly telling Salvador to pick any object enforcing the power he has. Salvador refuses and Cayo picks a woman statue to give to him. Salvador loudly says no and breaks it; when this occurs Madeinusa turns to see them. As a result of the broken statue, Cayo warns him that he will not take anything from his home. The broken statue represents the father's view of women: motionless beings whose actions are controlled by men. The father thinks that Madeinusa was pressured into having intercourse with Salvador and tells him, "la rompiste" [you broke her or ruined her] when in reality it was Madeinusa who willingly had sex; she chose to disobey Cayo and the town's expectations during Holy Time. The scene concludes with a long shot of Madeinusa staring into the camera, she seems hopeless as she is surrounded by religious and other objects. Her ambition to escape her town appears distant for she is locked away, but that is not an obstacle in reaching her goal of escaping to Lima.

Throughout the film Salvador gives the impression of being the savior for Madeinusa, honoring the meaning of his name. Being a foreigner from Lima, Madeinusa believes he is destined to save her and take her to the capital where her mother lives (Holmes 208). She, however, can save herself. She endures various events that ultimately lead her to murder her father and finally be free to travel to Lima. After witnessing Cayo's destruction of a pair of earrings, the only and most precious belonging she had inherited from her mother, she decides to finally stop being under her father's control and become the owner of her own life and body. Through Madeinusa's actions, Llosa disrupts the heteropatriarchal and religious oppressive systems that continue to monitor the behavior of the women of this town.

In one crucial scene, the first shot uses low-key lighting to display darkness on half of Madeinusa's face in order to signify the sinister act she is about to commit. She makes her father's favorite chicken soup and adds rat poison to it. As she is preparing the dish, she sings a song in Quechua about escaping during Holy Time, which completely relates to her life at this moment. Once again, half of Madeinusa is lit in a close-up shot of her face once she has finished the chicken soup and is calling her father to eat as she hides her true intentions. The event of her murdering Cayo alternates with different scenes in the town where the girls are singing that Holy Time is over and a man is uncovering Jesus' eyes. It is at this moment where the audience is witnessing how religion is no longer controlling Madeinusa.

The entire scene of the father dying is seen through a mirror. The use of the mirror inevitably highlights a reflection of what the protagonist wants, her actions, and the possible consequences. The first time Madeinusa appears in the mirror, she kisses her father on the lips just like she did when she kissed Jesus before his death earlier in the film. This action being placed in the mirror reveals how she is finally free. Madeinusa can now do as she pleases without being limited or reprimanded by her father, who previously represented Jesus. The mirror also highlights Salvador's horrified face since he has witnessed the murder and the shot changes focus from Madeinusa to him. He calls her crazy because she killed her father because he broke her mother's earrings. With the close-ups to her face, she demonstrates guilt for possibly being caught, but still believes that she made the correct choice claiming "Me rompió mis aretes [he broke my earrings]." One crucial moment in the scene occurs when the camera moves to a close-up shot of Salvador removing Madeinusa's plastic gloves. By doing it, metaphorically he exposes how Madeinusa transfers the blame to him. An act of comfort and solidarity turns into one of backstabbing and his entrapment in the town. Chale, Madeinusa's sister, arrives at the house and sees her father dead, and similarly to Jesus, she closes his eyes. Llosa continues to highlight the freedom of male figures in the lives of these girls and women. The ultimate moment of Madeinusa's true freedom and empowerment arrives when Chale accuses el gringo, Salvador, of killing her father. Madeinusa quickly joins Chale and thereby seals her fate of freedom. Her actions can be read with "a postcolonial feminist framework as radical acts of self-realization which established conditions for personal freedom" (Palaversich 497).

Salvador turns into the scapegoat for Madeinusa. Although he does not save her as his name would suggest, he unwillingly takes the blame for her crime. The death of Christ, represented by Cayo's death, and Salvador's punishment all played a part in allowing Madeinusa to become more mobile and she ultimately can travel to Lima as she desired. Cayo's death liberated her from the heteropatriarchal system and Salvador's punishment freed her from the colonial power he represented. Madeinusa's journey is not to enter into a more civilized city, it is one of initiation and having the power to create her own identity in another place (Palaversich 501). In this sense, the film reflects on and highlights the various strategies that empower Claudia Llosa's female characters.

Bibliography

"Claudia Llosa." <Https://womenmakefilm.tcm.com/filmmaker/claudia-llosa/.
Holmes, Amanda. "Gender and Nature in Madeinusa (2006)." *Revista Canadiense de Estudios Hispánicos,* vol. 37, no.1, Otoño 2012, pp. 204–216.
Ortner, Sherry B. *The Politics and Erotics of Culture*, Bacon Press, 1997.
Palaverish, Diana. "Cultural Dyslexia and the Politics of Cross-cultural Excursion in Claudia Llosa's Madeinusa." *The Bulletin of Hispanic Studies*, Vol. 90, No.4, January 2013, pp. 489-503.

CHAPTER 5

Qué Tan Lejos (Tania Hermida. 2006, Ecuador)

Abstract An innovative take on the road movie genre, *Qué Tan Lejos* portrays the relationship between two women with opposite personalities, Tristeza (Sadness) and Esperanza (Hope), while traveling. The chapter's objective is to analyze how the director Tania Hermida recreates the road movie not only as a genre in which growth and maturity are achieved by the characters but also as a genre in which gender solidarity is explored. The solidarity between these women develops without any male love interests in sight. Although Tristeza's travel is motivated by a man (she wants to stop her ex-boyfriend's wedding), Hermida's perspective on women moves them beyond the "whys" to focus on the "how" and their discoveries. Her conversations are political, tender, and nostalgic, providing the protagonists with a space to define themselves by their own company.

Keywords Road movie • Traveling • Touristic • Womanhood • Friendship • Ecuadorean cinema

© The Author(s), under exclusive license to Springer Nature Switzerland AG 2024
D. Abreu-Torres et al., *Latinidad and Film*,
https://doi.org/10.1007/978-3-031-56118-4_5

Production

Production	Corporación Ecuador para Largo
Screenplay	Tania Hermida
Producers	Tania Hermida, Gervasio Iglesias, Mary Palacios
Cinematography	Armando Salazar
Film Editing	Ivan Mora Manzano

Cast

Tristeza/Teresa	Cecilia Vallejo
Esperanza	Tania Martinez
Jesus	Pancho Aguirre
Andres	Fausto Miño

Synopsis

Esperanza and Tristeza meet each other on a bus that has to stop due to a protest. Esperanza is a Spanish tourist in Ecuador, trying to capture everything with her camera. Tristeza, whose real name is Teresa, is trying to stop the wedding of her on-and-off boyfriend. Together they start a journey that takes them to places in Ecuador that Esperanza did not think to visit and with which Tristeza had lost touch. Traveling from Quito to Cuenca, this unlikely couple of travelers will help and support each other to discover a better situation than they thought they were pursuing (Fig. 5.1).

Fig. 5.1 Esperanza and Tristeza traveling together

Director's Take: Tania Hermida (1969–)

Tania Hermida is a director, a scholar of cinema, an activist, and a teacher. From her most recent position as director of the Cinema School at Universidad de las Artes in Guayaquil, her goal is to distribute cinema's artistry through her teaching and research, but it must be a cinema that is not only for entertainment but that has a specific purpose. Her film *Qué Tan Lejos* is an illustration of this commitment, one that is influenced by her "ancestors," as she called them, the pioneers of the New Latin American Cinema (Nuevo Cine Latinoamericano) from the 1960s.

During the innovative decade of the 1960s, Latin American directors such as Glauber Rocha, Nelson Pereira Dos Santos, Julio García Espinosa, Tomás Gutiérrez Alea, and Fernando Birri created a cinema that went against Hollywood's guidelines and exhibited a new spirit of political commitment. It was a filmic sensitivity that was aware of the intricacies and complexities of the industry (creatively and economically) that did not rely on big production companies but rather in the belief in an independent system that would allow for new, creative freedom. According to Hermida, this New Latin American Cinema was not

> ni siquiera en su fundación … se propuso ser un cine ni dogmático, ni de propaganda, ni unívoco. Al contrario, las primeras películas [de esta época] … son películas extremadamente complejas, extremadamente artísticas, poéticas. Es decir, combinan este compromiso con su propia historia … y en ese sentido son políticas, pero al mismo tiempo son unas exploraciones estéticas, artísticas, tan hondas … que son arte. [not even when it was founded … it set out to be a cinema that was neither dogmatic, nor propaganda, nor unequivocal. On the contrary, the first films [of this era] … they are extremely complex films, extremely artistic, poetic. In other words, they combine this commitment with its own history … and in that sense they are political, but at the same time they are aesthetic, artistic explorations, so deep … that they are art]. (Telesur/YouTube 2018)

This appreciation of the New Latin American Cinema is what inspires Hermida to focus on stories that are personal and artistically attractive accounts about the political environment in Latin America, specifically in Ecuador. Hermida does not have a long filmography. Her two main feature films are narratives that have female protagonists who are agents of their own truth and actions. In *Qué Tan Lejos*, both Tristeza and Esperanza, although they have strayed from their main course, take action and do not wait for something to happen to them. Many times along their journey they are confronted with questions from male travelers about why they are traveling alone. Hermida understands how patriarchal society can be both traumatizing and subtle, and she prefers to play with the subtlety of two women traveling and how people react to them.

The director's cinematographic perspective of Ecuador, a mixture of panoramic views and attention to detail, creates a spatial sense that has been defined by critics both as a touristic advertisement and as an exploration of a deeper Ecuador, one not considered in newscasts or media narratives. Thus, Hermida's filmographic language is one committed to her personal space, Ecuador, and to her experience as a woman and one of the few successful female directors in a Latin American industry still struggling with diversity and gender equity. As she affirmed in an interview in 2014:

> Uno aprende una gramática básica en el proceso de formación académica, unos recursos técnicos, pero para aprender eso es manejar una gramática solamente, es como pensar que para ser poeta necesitas aprender una gramática escrita, pero de ahí no sale la poesía, la poesía viene en el momento en que tú te apropias del lenguaje y de alguna manera lo pones a decir desde tu experiencia, y ahí ya no hay gramática sino ruptura, diálogo, encuentro, inspiración; lo mismo es el cine [One learns a basic grammar in the process of academic training, some technical resources, but to learn that is to only learn how to handle a grammar, it is like thinking that to be a poet you need to learn a written grammar, but poetry does not come from there, poetry comes from the moment in which you own language and in some way you make it speak from your experience, and right then and then, there is no longer grammar but a rupture, a dialogue, an encounter, some inspiration; the same happens in cinema]. (Cited in Almachi-Barros, 41)

Film, then, is a poetic visualization of the experiences of the now, on how to reappropriate what was learned and make it one's own, a way to propel new representations in the future. Hermida is committed to that future.

COMMENTARY AND CONTEXT

Qué Tan Lejos premiered in 2006. The production of the film was a transitional piece that navigated a complex filmographic context. At first, there was no clear funding, but the director and the producers were able to hustle a total budget of $200,000.00 between state and private investors.

Although the 2006 cinema law, Ley de Fomento del Cine Nacional (Law to Promote National Cinema), did not impact the production, it influenced the distribution, particularly in Spain through the support of Ibermedia. Still, the film is not a big production but an independent effort to illustrate the hopes of a better Ecuador.

After the creation of free market trade between Latin America, the United States, and Europe in the 1990s, the continents suffered a pivotal change in labor, commercial exchanges, and communication. Latin America became the central generator of main resources, while the United States and Europe manufactured and innovated with these main resources. Thus, Ecuador, like many Latin American countries, suffered diminishing land ownership, privatization of the labor market, and lack of a safety net, particularly for the most marginalized, Indigenous, and peasant communities. This situation created a dangerous environment in which politics became polarized as many in the marginalized communities began to organize and protest against the government. From the beginning of the 2000s, Ecuador had four presidents with intermittent mandates—two years on average—until the presidency of Rafael Correa in 2007. About the connections between this political turmoil and *Qué Tan Lejos*, Hermida commented:

> Y se ven muchas cosas [en el film]: un país abandonado, del que, aparentemente, todos se han ido; en el que hay una huelga, pero nadie sabe bien por qué; en el que hay varias versiones de la realidad, pero ninguna coincide con la realidad. Es un país que no parece viable. *Qué tan lejos* se escribió en un Ecuador que acababa de dolarizarse ... Habían caído dos presidentes, y mientras filmábamos cayó el tercero. [And you see many things (in the film): an abandoned country, from which, apparently, everyone has left; in which there is a strike, but nobody really knows why; in which there are several versions of reality, but none of them coincide with reality. It is a country that does not seem viable. *Qué tan lejos* was written in an Ecuador that had just become dollarized ... Two presidents had fallen, and while we were filming the third one fell]. (Cabrera Kozisek, www.eltelegrafo.com)

The film does not represent the political aspect of Ecuador, we do not see the turmoil nor the migrations, but it is all there in the silence and vastness of the space, almost empty, almost with no one to help.

In order to explore the physical and psychological spaces of Ecuador and the characters in the film, the director constructs a narrative based on the road movie genre. Esperanza and Tristeza start their traveling with different goals but come together in the knowledge the journey provides to them. At the beginning, it seems as if the film will have a concrete journey between point A and point B. In the in-between, however, there are detours and a variety of ways of traveling in which both women begin to know each other and forge a relationship.

Before the journey begins, Hermida provides a space for reflection on their transitional situation. While waiting for the bus, Tristeza is reading *El mono gramatical* by Octavio Paz. The quote that we can hear deals with the importance of naming but also how naming is deceiving. Whatever something is, it is out there: "Estas palabras que escribo andan en busca de su sentido y en esto consiste todo su sentido. El sentido no está en el texto, sino afuera [These words I write are in search of their meaning and in this consists all their sense of existing. The meaning is not in the text, but outside of it]" (*Qué Tan Lejos*). To some extent, Hermida is signaling how Tristeza is searching for a new name, a new identity, although this is still unknown to her. The quote, however, provides depth to the journey: is not about traveling but about looking for meaning out there, in what can be seen and experienced.

Esperanza has a similar sentiment and approach in the film when, after trying to engage Tristeza in a conversation, Tristeza instead gives her a book to read. The book is *Sor Juana Inés de la Cruz y las trampas de la fe*, also authored by Octavio Paz. What Esperanza reads is another key from the director to foreshadow how the character's travels will change: "Los libros del abuelo le abrieron las puertas de un mundo distinto... Un mundo masculino. La realidad es el lenguaje. Juana Inés habita la casa del lenguaje. Esa casa no está poblada por hombres o mujeres, sino por unas criaturas más reales, duraderas y consistentes que todas las realidades y que todos los seres de carne y hueso: las ideas [Her grandfather's books opened the doors to a different world ... A masculine world. Reality is language. Juana Inés inhabits the house of language. That house is not inhabited by men or women, but by creatures more real, lasting and consistent than all realities and all beings of flesh and blood: ideas]" (*Qué Tan Lejos*). While Tristeza's reading implied for her to get out there, this quote from *Sor Juana* is asking Esperanza to be more introspective, to be aware that what she sees may have multiple meanings and multiple ways to be interpreted. Thus, through books and language, Hermida provides a more philosophical perspective for both characters and a more significant journey in which both Esperanza and Tristeza will be able to bond and learn from each other.

Books are not the only extradiegetic resource Hermida uses to differentiate her take on the road movie genre. There is also a female narrator who provides the spectator with some more information about the characters. As a footnote in a book, a female voice gives personal details of Tristeza and Esperanza, such as full name, who were their parents, what age they were when they had their first menstruation, and what familial pathologies are relevant to their physical or mental health. It is not a voice that cares about the women, but an omniscient narrator that is able to convey some concrete information with which the spectator can make their own conclusions about them. These details are provided in parallel scenes in which each character is in front of a public bathroom mirror as if whatever their public persona may be is not the reality that they are, or, at least, that their personal history offers. Similar to the book quotes, the narrator, although distant and cold in tone, is contextualizing the journey and deepening the characters' inner space in order to make sense of the outer space they will encounter. The encounter with the expanse of Ecuador, however, turns out to be more complicated. Soon after the bus trip begins, it needs to stop. An Indigenous protest is happening and has closed all the main highways. What looked like a certain path starts to change course and such is Tristeza and Esperanza's journey.

A Touristic Site

At the beginning of the film, we see Esperanza arriving in Ecuador as a tourist. We can see her calmness when looking around and breathing in the view. This calmness, however, is short-lived. The taxi driver tries to take advantage of her as a tourist, particularly as someone from Spain, billing a high payment for the ride from the airport. Esperanza tries to be polite and asks him why the high price. The taxi driver cannot provide concrete facts about the billing but starts saying that he knows she has money as his cousin living in Spain has informed him that many Spaniards are living very well. Esperanza tries to explain she is not like other Spaniards and pays him what is expected. The taxi driver gets angry and leaves. This first interaction with Ecuador transforms Esperanza's touristic body as a representation of an imperial attitude toward the visiting country: her visit is an enjoyment, a pleasurable journey that sees Ecuador as something to consume. After their meeting on the bus, Tristeza reminds Esperanza, constantly, that she cannot see Ecuador only through her camera lens, but that she needs to look and learn, to see Ecuador beyond the tourist attractions:

> Esperanza is the foreign visitor, whose "tourist gaze" is foregrounded right from the very start ... somewhat imposingly requests [to Tristeza] to exchange seats so that she can sit near the window and film interesting locations from the bus ... Teresa, on the contrary, is the "local" visitor, who has her eyes (hidden behind glasses) firmly fixed on a book by Octavio Paz. ("Countering the Tourist Gaze," n.p.)

This interpretation of how Hermida treats the touristic gaze in a road film may seem paradoxical or misplaced. Still, there is more to it. Similar to *Motorcycle Diaries*, another Latin American film, Hermida's use of panoramic views of Ecuador has been interpreted as purposefully touristic. As an online reviewer states: "If there were ever a movie made specifically to help me in my goal of getting a glimpse of a country, it's this one. This is a road trip movie, and as such, it provides many shots of Ecuador's stunning vistas along the 265-mile route from Quito to Cuenca" (travelingbyfilm.wordpress.com).

The road trip, then, is a twofold guide: it provides insight into a journey but also works as a postcard that allows the spectator to plan and dream about traveling to Ecuador. That may be the case, however, the relationship between the plot and the scenery is not as clear-cut as it may seem. While Esperanza arrives in Ecuador as a tourist, her encounter with Teresa disarms this reality. As Marcelo Báez comments in his analysis of *Qué Tan Lejos* and *Y tu mamá también*: "En ambos filmes la naturaleza no es un monumento simbólico, mucho menos es una representación de lo nacional, con ese postalismo que buscaba proyectar un potencial turístico repitiendo los discursos modernizantes de los estados-nación colonizadores. El paisaje en el cine latinoamericano del nuevo siglo es un espacio especular donde priman las incógnitas en vez de las respuestas" "[In both films, nature is not a symbolic monument, much less is it a representation of what is national, with that postalism that sought to project a potential tourism by repeating the modernizing discourses of the colonizing nation-states. The landscape in the Latin American cinema of the new century is a specular space where the unknowns prevail instead of the answers]" (32). The Ecuadorian scenery that the protagonists travel and visit is usually empty and desolate as if asking not only where the people are but what has happened to them. Again, Hermida brings the political not by force but implicated in her framing of the journey. The journey for Esperanza starts with a touristic purpose that needs to be disarmed. Teresa is the person to constantly question her and provides a deeper understanding of what to see and how to see it. Teresa's gaze then is also repurposed: she is now looking out from a book. Esperanza's gaze, thus, is turned inward; it becomes reflective.

Ecuador from a Distance

Tristeza and Esperanza's traveling becomes a zig-zagging of modes of transportation after their bus is stopped by a protest. We do not see the protest but only know about it by information received from the characters. Both women decide to subsequently travel in an open caravan, in the back of a pick-up truck, by hitch-hiking, on a motorcycle, and by horse. Their objective is to get to Cuenca, for Tristeza's benefit and Esperanza's adventure. Along the way, the Ecuadorian panoramic views open, but we do not see the majestic parts of Ecuador—most of it is covered with mist and rainy days—but instead we see the smaller places: towns, farmlands, and plazas. Just like Esperanza's hope to see the volcanoes, the spectator is left with the need to see more. This desire may be the motivation for some critics to describe this film as touristic, but tourism never happens. What happens is the encounter with individuals that elicit reflections from the main characters.

When traveling down a highway in the back of a pick-up truck owned by two newsmen, the truck suddenly stops. The reporter and his cameraman start filming what seems to be debris from the protest. While the reporter announces how the Indigenous protest is causing damages and confirms with Esperanza how she was derailed from her travel to Cuenca, Tristeza says that she was in support of the protest and that it seems it had already moved on. She is cut from the interview and the reporter finishes his video. In a subtle way, the film establishes a positionality through Tristeza but does not take a concrete political view. It is admitting how Ecuador's economic benefit from tourism may be impacted, while also acknowledging the urgency of the Indigenous movement and legitimizing their strategy. This moment allows for both women to bond as well. Tristeza tries to convince the reporter to drive them to the nearest city that keeps them on their route to Cuenca. When this request is denied, Tristeza decides to continue by foot, convincing Esperanza by reminding her that she cannot stay alone with the drivers. Esperanza trusts Tristeza who is happy to guide her. Through this half of the trip, both have encountered a partner in each other and they continue their mutual support needed to accomplish their respective goals.

While walking, the women meet a new traveling companion, Jesús, who arrives at the moment Esperanza is sharing how at some point in her traveling she started to feel lost. He becomes a kind of compass they can use in order to secure their trip. When they finally arrive in a small town, it is completely empty. The entire scene of the plaza and the mountains in the background offers a perfect perspective for the spectator and Esperanza to enjoy. The place, however, feels like a ghost town, as if no one were living there. Esperanza still wants to visit a tourist site and is annoyed when neither Jesús nor Tristeza shows any excitement at her suggestion. Jesús then explains that he is not traveling for pleasure but that he needs to take his grandmother's ashes to Cuenca as soon as possible. Esperanza apologizes and sees this as another way to remind her and the spectators that this journey that we are witnessing is not a touristic one but a closer look at Ecuador and the small actions that happen throughout the country. By relegating the protest to an invisible background, Hermida is able to focus on small details and on small stories.

Qué Tan Lejos is a different type of road film. By the end, the protagonists have evolved and a friendship is born, but their arrival at point B, Cuenca, triggers a new journey back home, to Quito. It becomes the start of a new process for both: for Tristeza is the assurance that she is more than her identity as a girlfriend; for Esperanza, traveling is not only big sites and tourism. As the director affirmed in an interview:

> Sigo convencida de que es una película con un lenguaje muy personal, lo que pasa es que eso conectó con el público, y creo que fue porque estábamos viviendo un sentimiento similar, de ser personajes de un país abandonado, de vivir con esa paradoja en un lugar que amamos pero al mismo tiempo no entendemos y a ratos odiamos. [I remain convinced that it is a film with a very personal language, what happens is that it connected with the public, and I think it was because we were experiencing a similar feeling, of being characters from an abandoned country, of living with that paradox in a place that we love but at the same time we do not understand and at times we hate]. (www.eltelegrafo.com, n.p.)

Through the perspective of two women, one an outsider and another an insider, Hermida is able to demonstrate the intricacies of the country of

Ecuador and of Ecuadorian identity and how the scenery that defines both is not enough. A journey to the knowledge of oneself is needed and the female protagonists are the best vessels to guarantee this self-acknowledgment. Alone in a road movie that could have been a dangerous path for both, Hermida lifts this tension through their solidarity and sense of purpose.

Bibliography

Almachi Barros, Silvia del Pilar. *Cine Ecuatoriano y Comunicación: Análisis narrativo de la película "Qué tan lejos" dirigida por Tania Hermida*. Trabajo de grado previa a la obtención del título de Comunicadora Social, Universidad Central del Ecuador, Quito, Ecuador, 2015. http://www.dspace.uce.edu.ec/handle/25000/4847. Accessed September 2022.

Báez Meza, Marcelo. "Y tu mamá también de Alfonso Cuarón y Qué tan lejos de Tania Hermida: dos españolas en la re-conquista fallida." *Fuera de Campo*, Vol. 2, No. 1, 2018, pp. 10-39.

Cabrera Kozisek, José Miguel. "Tania Hermida: Pensamos en el cine ecuatoriano como si hubiera empezado hace diez años." *El Telégrafo*, https://www.eltelegrafo.com.ec/noticias/carton/1/tania-hermida-pensamos-en-el-cine-ecuatoriano-como-si-hubiera-empezado-hace-diez-anos. Accessed September, 2022.

Hermida, Tania. "En Clave Política: Conversamos con Tania Hermida." *DailyMotion*, uploaded by TeleSur TV, 2019, https://www.dailymotion.com/video/x6ymezt.

Lie, Nadia. "Countering the Tourist Gaze: Que tan lejos (Tania Hermida, 2006)." *The Latin American (Counter-) Road Movie and Ambivalent Modernity*, Ebrary.net, https://ebrary.net/44172/economics/countering_tourist_gaze_lejos_tania_hermida_2006#985, Accessed July 16 2021.

PART III

Breaking the Binary

CHAPTER 6

La Mission (Peter Bratt, 2009, USA)

Abstract This chapter examines Peter Bratt's *La Mission* which proposes a thorough reflection on one of the most complex aspects of Latinx cultures: the multiple and somewhat contradictory definitions of masculinity. This analysis includes some of the traits in Bratt's independent cinematic production such as the economic and social struggles of today's Latinx communities in the United States, the use of intersectionality as a filmmaking approach, and the impact of the director's personal experience in the development of a cinema that speaks from the margins. The chapter highlights the discursive and visual resources utilized to ponder the constraining definitions of masculinity that traditionally have been present in U.S. Latinx communities. In this sense, the film challenges not only the use of violence as domination, but also the behaviors that assert an individual as masculine, as well as the discourses and practices that have oppressed those who break with the heterosexual compulsion historically associated with the U.S. Latinx experience.

Keywords Masculinity • Toxic masculinity • LGBTQ • Latinx community • Latino cinema

Production

Production	5 Stick Films
Director	Peter Bratt
Producers	Alpita Patel and Benjamin Bratt
Screenwriter	Peter Bratt
Director of Photography	Hiro Narita
Editor	Stan Webb

Cast

Che Rivera	Benjamin Bratt
Jesse Rivera	Jeremy Ray Valdez
Lena	Erika Alexander
Rene	Jesse Borrego
Ana	Talisa Soto
Jordan	Max Rosenak

Synopsis

Che Rivera, the protagonist, is a single father, an ex-alcoholic, and an ex-convict who lives in the Mission District of San Francisco, California, with his son Jesse. Che is respected and admired for being an old-school ex-gang member and for his talent with lowrider cars. Jesse is in his last year of high school and is preparing to go to college in Los Angeles. He is a good student and his father is proud of him. When Che learns that Jesse is gay, he has difficulty accepting this fact and kicks him out of the house. The closeness between father and son is broken by Che's homophobia. Lena, the new neighbor, has an alternative lifestyle that is non-conformist and challenges Che's macho attitude and helps him see the damage he causes in not accepting his son fully.

Director: Peter Bratt (1962–)

Born in the Mission District of San Francisco in 1962, Peter Bratt grew up in a tough and historic time for Latinxs in the United States. During this time, people were fighting for their civil rights as citizens in this country. His family experience, with an Anglo-American father and a Peruvian mother, was a strong influence on the development of his work as a filmmaker. His mother is an Indigenous activist and participated in the movement for the rights of Native Americans. Bratt, along with his siblings, attended political rallies with her from a young age. He grew up around people from different cultures but did not experience seeing such ethnic diversity on the screen; therefore, he became interested in telling the stories of the people he knew. In his films, he draws attention to difficult topics that an audience might not necessarily want to watch, but, ultimately, he intends to provoke a conversation about these important issues.

Bratt graduated from Cowell College at the University of California, Santa Cruz. In 1996 he directed his first feature, *Follow Me Home*. With this film, he began to work on the subject of race/ethnicity. *La Mission* (2009) is also concerned with the issue of race in a subtle way and focuses on the destructiveness of violence in the Latinx community. He is a Rockefeller fellow. For him, film production is an attempt to achieve social justice. This goal is portrayed by many of the issues in his work, including the intersection between identity, masculinity, gender, sexuality, and race. There are two influences that led him to become a filmmaker: the struggle for social justice and Native American spirituality. In 2017, he released *Dolores*, a documentary about the civil rights leader and icon Dolores Huerta. This film debuted at the Sundance Film Festival and won several awards, including a 2018 Peabody Award and a Critic's Circle Award.

Commentary and Context

The film was shot in the Mission District of San Francisco, where the Bratt brothers grew up. Historically, this community is the oldest neighborhood in the city, made up of working-class immigrants: first Europeans and then Chicanx and Latin Americans, starting in the 1960s. Since then, the district has had the largest population of Central Americans in the United States. Latinos were the majority of the ethnic composition until 2012. The district demographics began to change when businessmen, foreigners, hipsters, and people from the suburbs began to move into the Mission neighborhood. This is represented in the film with the character of Lena, who can be defined as a "hipster," but who also brings a feminist perspective to the plot.

The Mission District itself is a character in the film. Consisting of a working-class majority population, the location offers a great sense of this community of workers and street culture. For example, Che and his colleagues are bus drivers for public transportation. Not only are there visual representations of people but also of the buildings and murals that depict the history and culture of those living there. These murals and streets celebrate Latinx cultures but also protest the injustices in Central America and the United States against Indigenous peoples. In the film, we see many moments in which "los concheros," a group of people celebrating the Aztec dances and cosmovision, are dancing in the streets of the Mission District adding to its identity as a character.

Another identity represented is lowrider culture, which is a predominant part of the plot. This culture began in the southern suburbs of Los Angeles, California, in the early 1950s and became popular about four decades before the film, in the 1970s. It expresses the pride and joy of the Chicanx or Mexican-American—as well as African-American—communities while protesting against assimilation into Eurocentric, Anglo-dominant U.S. culture. Traditionally, men dominate lowrider communities, since they are the ones who work on the lowrider cars and show them off. Cruising is an important aspect of this culture. It is a social event where people gather with their vehicles to drive *low and slow*: low for the lowness of the cars, and slow for their speed on the streets. In the film, the character of Che epitomizes lowriders and demonstrates that the culture is still active. The people of this district have maintained their role in it since many of them work on their cars and show them off in public when they ride them. Che's character involvement in such culture represents a big aspect of his masculine identity.

Masculinity features prominently in this film, both in the thematic and visual aspects. For the U.S. mainstream and Latinx cultures, masculinity defines a man as dominant, aggressive, and violent, but at the same time as responsible and respectful (Mirandé 69). The relevant aspect of this film is that it not only denounces "hegemonic masculinity" (Connell 1985) but also makes explicit the many versions of masculine identity. As Nikki Wedgood (2009) proposes, it is necessary to address the moments in which toxic/hegemonic masculinity is subverted through different cultural practices that, in the end, demonstrate that masculinity is not equivalent to violence and dominance. *La Mission*, by itself, represents a big departure from the traditional models of masculinity offered by U.S. mainstream culture, especially in the representation of Latinx masculine characters. For this film, it will be crucial to disidentify Latino men with the stereotypical version of hegemonic and toxic masculinity. *La Mission* proposes more nuanced versions of this identity, bringing to the cultural arena a refreshing perspective.

Che's Trouble with Alternative Masculinities

Che, the protagonist, is strong and independent. He is someone who cares for his family as a provider. Some of the negative characteristics of his masculinity are that he is sexist, homophobic, and can become intemperate. In one scene, Che violently confronts Jesse, his son, about the photographs he found of him in a gay club with an Anglo "friend." As an old-school Chicano, Che is respected in the streets and uses physical violence to solve his problems. While, on the other hand, Jesse represents a different masculine identity that queers the notion of Latinx hypermasculinity. In this sense, Jesse's body conveys that "Based on the premise that bodies are both objects and agents of practice, [...] the relationship between the body and the social is two-way and simultaneous and how practice itself is informed by the structures within which bodies are appropriated and defined" (Connell 91). Jesse has two sides to his character; he wants to be cool and visibly masculine, according to the Latino cultural imaginary, as seen with his wardrobe and how he carries himself, but he also represents an alternative sexual identity, which differs from the ideal model of masculinity according to traditional Latinx values.

This scene depicts, visually and through dialogue, the confrontation between father and son; each one has a different version of what it means to be a "good man." At this moment, Che is confronting his son because he found some pictures of Jesse and his friend kissing each other at a gay bar in the Castro district, San Francisco. With the use of low-angle shots, the film focuses on Che and the relationship dynamics with his son. These shots depict him as the dominant character. His body seems menacing as he is looking over Jesse, yelling, and beating him. His son just sits there accepting his insults and receiving the abuse.

The visual language of this scene is powerful. With the medium shots that follow in this scene, an aggressive tone is set. Che's emotions also emphasize the ambiance of this scene that matches the red color of the room demonstrating the anger and other strong emotions he feels when he learns about his son's sexuality. Jesse is sitting in a corner engulfed by red walls. In a heteropatriarchal society, a traditional male solves his problems with violence. As such, we observe Che violently beating his son because this situation embarrasses Che and goes against his traditional, conservative idea of what is a masculine man. This is the first time that Jesse cannot deny he is gay and he is helpless. Throughout the film, however, both characters will undergo an important transformation. In this sense, the film opens new spaces for LGBTQ+ communities, especially in the notion of respect for different sexual and affective identities.

Differing Opinions Over the Acceptance of Queer Identities

This film is challenging, through several characters, the compulsory heterosexuality that pervades our society. At the same time, as Venkatesh proposes about queer Latin American cinema, it indeed questions the sociocultural dynamics that are embedded in the notion of compulsory heterosexuality and at the same time "encourages viewership and the circulation of empathy" (61) for the queer characters. Along with the challenge of traditional Latino masculinity, the film presents queer identities from a deep perspective. Che does not accept Jesse's queer sexuality and his reaction is different from that of other supportive family members. Performing a different version of Latino masculinity, Jesse's uncle, René, accepts him immediately. He is caring toward his nephew and his own children. In his house, we see an environment of respect toward women and other identities. It is noteworthy that René is not only short physically, but he has a different performance of masculinity through his body. While Che's body is shown in several scenes while boxing, evoking his hard and resilient body, René's body is depicted as taking care of the children and driving an SUV, which is considered a typical "mother's" car. His body and masculine performance break the traditional masculine boundaries of the dominant society. As Nikki Wedwood (2009) has argued, we can emphasize the subversion of hegemonic masculinity to highlight more spaces within the film that bring acceptance to democratic models of Latino masculine identity.

Jesse is another character who subverts the traditional gender model that his father embodies. Like his uncle René, he is caring toward the people that surround him and values education instead of only focusing on lowriding culture. The film emphasizes his fears, dreams, emotions, and affectivity and offers a thoughtful young gay male representation as an example of how the film creates more complex characters. For instance, his masculinity is represented in the way in which he presents his body, and he aesthetically follows the Latinx codes of male fashion from his cultural environment. *La Mission* plays with the spectators at the beginning of the film as we see Jesse in a sequence that follows the stereotypical codes of Latino representation by mass media. We see him at his high school saying hi to his friends who are in a car as they are interrupted by a policeman. A few scenes later, Jesse arrives in a wealthy area of town and enters a house by simply opening the door and the camera focuses on his hand as he grabs a gun. The music that accompanies this sequence is intense: our emotions are heightened by the images and the music. A few seconds after Jesse grabs the gun, a white young man, only wearing a towel, is approaching him, emphasizing his vulnerable body. Jesse begins to talk aggressively to the "white boy" who is supposed to give Jesse "something" he does not have. The exchange ends with Jesse saying: "Your ass is mine," and the boy, with a big smile, tells him "I think I like the sound of that." The sequence drastically changes the tone with the smile and the kiss they give each other, indicating that everything was a performance, a (sexual) game between the two of them. Later, the spectators know that these two men are in love and certainly committed as a couple despite both being so young. Jordan—the whiteboy—is the one who drives Jesse to UCLA for a visit, also stays with him in the hospital while Jesse recovers from a shot wound, and finally, takes him to his own house to stay after the hospital, moment in which Che and Jesse rupture their relationship because of the father's homophobia. At the end of the film, we do not know if they are still together as a couple, but the film remarkably normalizes the two young men in love while breaking the visual codes that have characterized the representation of Latinos and gay characters in the media.

A final, and more conclusive, break with gender representations happens with the transformation of Che. After he discovers that Jesse is gay, Jesse is harassed at school and in the streets until he is shot. His son's hospitalization provokes Che to be more present as a father. After trying to force Jesse to return to live with him, Che breaks all contact with him and destroys the lowrider car that would have been his son's graduation present. Jesse graduates from high school and goes to college in Los Angeles, which greatly affects Che, although he refuses to admit it. There is a noticeable change in his appearance after Jesse leaves, as before Che was interested in looking good and his clothes were also well selected for his style. The audience can witness Che's vulnerability to the point where he begins drinking again. In this sequence, enacted as if it were an Indigenous ritual with images of conchero dancers, Che experiences a visible transformation. While he is walking with a bottle of alcohol, he is witness to a scene that will change his perspective completely: he sees a mother mourning the death of her son. The young man in question is actually the same one who shot Jesse. Che remains in front of the altar that has some pictures of the boy at different ages and begins to remember everything that happened. This montage serves as a reflection of who he was and his expectations as a parent. He leaves the bottle of alcohol he had bought and walks away with the determination to recover his son. The pre-Columbian music and dance serve as the rhythm of the sequence which is visually innovative because it combines several factors that are in the life of the protagonists: a strong sense of ethnic and cultural pride, but also an idiosyncrasy that is harmful to the people who dare to break the cultural norms, especially of gender and sexuality. The rain that accompanies the sequence symbolizes the beginning of something new, like the recently developed, stronger relationship between Che and Jesse. Water is used as a renewal and a cleansing for Che. The film does not present a clear and happy ending, but it invokes a new beginning. While driving to Los Angeles with the lowrider that has been completely restored, Che is moving forward, literally and figuratively, while attempting to start over with his son.

Bibliography

Connell, R.W. & Messerschmidt, James W. Hegemonic. "Masculinities: Rethinking the Concept." *Gender & Society*, Vol. 19, No. 6, Dec 2005. pp. 829–59.

Solis, Gabriel. "The Revolutionary History of Lowriders," 2017. www.vice.com.

Garofoli, Joe, Said Carolyn. "A Changing Mission: To Whom Does San Francisco's Oldest Neighborhood Belong?" *San Francisco Chronicle.* >www.sfchronicle.com/themissiom/a-changingmission.

Johnson, Reed. "Peter and Benjamin Bratt are on a mission." *Los Angeles Times,* Apr 2010. >www.latimes.com/archives/la-xpm-2010-apr-10-la-et-bratt10-2010apr-story.html.

Mirandé, Alfredo. *Hombres y Machos: Masculinity and Latino Culture.* Boulder; Westview Press, 1997.

Rodriguez, Angel. "Gay in the Latino Community: A Film Review of 'La Mission'." *Latino Rebels,* Apr 2013. www.latinorebels.com/2013/04/17/gay-in-the-latino-communities-a-film-review-of-la-mission/

"Peter Bratt, 'La Mission': Patriarch, Homosexual and Change." *Indiewire,* Jan 2009.

Venketash, Vinodh. *New Maricón Cinema.* University of Texas Press, 2016.

Wedgwood, Nicki. "Connell's theory of masculinity—its origins and influences on the study of gender." The Journal of Gender Studies, vol. 18, no. 4, 2009, pp. 329–339.

CHAPTER 7

Entre Nos (Paola Mendoza and Gloria La Morte. 2009, USA)

Abstract *Entre Nos* is the personal portrayal of a Colombian immigrant family struggling to survive in New York City. Based on the experiences of Paola Mendoza (co-director with Gloria La Morte), the film is an intimate representation of Mariana, a woman who becomes empowered and resilient, after her husband abandons her shortly after arriving in the United States. With a tourist visa that will soon expire, Mariana's possibilities for employment are limited and become nulled when her husband leaves her and their two children. She must overcome the emotional and physical abandonment by being strong for her children, being creative with their financial limitations as a family, and focusing on the positive aspects of life as they navigate their challenging new world. The aspects analyzed in this chapter synthesize Mendoza and La Morte's vision of this particular story of strength and resiliency via a personal gaze that explores an immigrant woman's story of survival.

Keywords Immigration • Family • Motherhood • Latino cinema • Coming of age

Production

Production	IndiePix Studios, Lucky Hat Entertainment, Rola Productions, La Morte/Skolnik
Directors	Paola Mendoza and Gloria La Morte
Producers	Bob Alexander, executive producer; Steve Bannatyne, executive producer; Alexander Bing, associate producer; Ryan Harrington, executive producer; Joseph La Morte, producer; María Neyla Santa María, associate producer; Michael Skolnik, producer; Genna Terranova, executive producer
Screenwriters	Paola Mendoza and Gloria La Morte
Director of Photography	Bradford Young
Film Editing	Gloria La Morte

Cast

Mariana	Paola Mendoza
Gabriel	Sebastián Villada
Andrea	Laura Montana
Joe	Anthony Chisholm
Antonio	Andrés Munar
Preet	Sarita Choudhury
Mi-Sun	Isabel Sung

Synopsis

Mariana is a Colombian new immigrant in New York City. She arrived with her husband after he found a job in Brooklyn, New York, bringing her kids, Gabriel, 10, and Andrea, 6, with them. What seems to be a happy beginning for her family, becomes a nightmare for Mariana. At the start of the summer, her husband abandons her after supposedly accepting a new job in Miami, leaving her with no money and no prospects on how to move forward in her new life. Mariana needs to overcome unemployment, eviction, homelessness, and uncertainty along with her children. After hitting rock bottom and with the help of allies she finds along the way, she is able to get ahead and procure a better future for herself and her children (Fig. 7.1).

Fig. 7.1 Gabriel, Mariana, and Andrea

Director's Take: Paola Mendoza (1981–) and Gloria La Morte (1981–)

Paola Mendoza was born in Bogota, Colombia, but arrived in the United States when she was a young girl. Gloria La Morte is from Hackensack, New Jersey, the daughter of Colombian parents. Both women bring their experiences as part of the Colombian diaspora to their films, focusing on themes related to diversity, racial discrimination, poverty, marginalization, and resilience. Mendoza studied theater at UCLA and received her master's from Sarah Lawrence College in New York. She fell in love with film when she had the opportunity to act and be an active participant in the development of *On the Outs* (2004), an experience she describes as her film school, which led her to direct *Autumn's Eyes* (2006), a documentary that follows a young girl whose mother has been incarcerated. Many of the themes in *Autumn's Eyes* are also developed in *Entre Nos*, particularly motherhood, the struggle of women of color, community support, and resiliency. After *Entre Nos,* Mendoza became involved in cultural activism, focusing on immigration and women's rights, both through media and film. A highlight of her activism was her participation in the 2017 Women's March (a reaction to the 2016 Elections in which Donald Trump became president). She was a cultural representative, preparing a lineup of artists, stars, and social activists in the arts that consolidated the women's movement. She followed up on this work by bringing awareness, via social media and a short film, to the separation of families that happened after the zero-tolerance policy on immigration under the Trump administration in 2018.

Gloria La Morte started her film career as a producer, actor, and writer of the short film *Details* (2000), acquired by HBO, in which a woman is deciding to end or continue her unsatisfying life. Framed as a dark comedy, La Morte explores depression, family ties, compromise, and gender expectations, paving the way for her work with Mendoza. She graduated from William Paterson University in New Jersey and founded the production company Joeyngloria with her editor and producer husband, Joseph La Morte. At the beginning of Joeyngloria, La Morte collaborated with Mendoza on the edition of *Autumn's Eyes*, and due to this collaboration Mendoza and La Morte realized their work together had just begun. Through the work of her production company, she has fomented Latinx voices by working with big firms like HBO and Netflix in the creation of programming that appeals to and represents this population, either through short films, mini-docs, or web series, also with the participation of Mendoza. Both creators found their voices by writing their way into film and production, creating the space that allowed for the development of *Entre Nos*.

Commentary and Context

Entre Nos began when Mendoza and La Morte finished the production and distribution of *Autumn's Eyes*. Mendoza proposed the script idea to her partner, based on Mendoza's mother's experience in the United States, and they began developing the feature-length film. For two years they debated ideas and scenes and finally submitted the script to the Independent Film Project (IFP). The script was accepted in the competition and also won an award for best script, which was a critical step as the prize came with a financial packet available to be used within two years. This legitimization of their work allowed Mendoza and La Morte to look for more financial support. Through Tribeca, the writers, now producers, were able to secure film equipment that fast-tracked the production and they started to film for almost three weeks (18 days) in Jackson Heights, where an important Colombian community has been established.

With a clear objective to portray the Latinx community, especially in Jackson Heights, in the most credible way, these filmmakers included community participation in the production. Neighbors were extras, set designer helpers, technical interns, and part of the catering team. The most crucial participation of the community was through casting. Mendoza did not want professional child actors, as she wanted to portray raw emotions from them, which meant that they needed to do an open casting. They found many good actors from various places in New York, but it was not until the Colombian parade in Jackson Heights that she was able to find the child who would portray Gabriel and later, she decided who would play the character of Andrea. These decisions were made close to the start of the production, preparing the kids for their roles simultaneously with them on film.

Both Mendoza and La Morte directed the film, constructing a peculiar perspective of a Latina single mother of two not as a victim of her circumstances but as an agent of change. As women directors, they were aware of the romanticism an immigration story might offer. They decided to present a story colored not in Black or white issues, but in a gray area that would speak more of their participants than the politics that brought them to a precarious situation. Mariana was a victim of the lack of immigration reform, but she did not stop to fix the small things that would allow her family to belong to the United States.

Produced in 2008, at the beginning of the Obama administration, the context in which the film was finally recreated was hopeful. Mendoza and La Morte viewed immigration as an important issue to be discussed, but one in which political considerations were too limited to the stereotypical immigrants from Mexico or Central/South America who cross the border with minimal education and resources. In *Entre Nos*, another face of immigration is represented. With a tourist visa, the main character is able to arrive and start a new life with her husband, wishfully thinking he would be able to claim her and their children through his work visa, and later open the possibility of obtaining a green card. Due to her husband's abandonment, however, Mariana is left undocumented, without the possibility of legal work. In the margins of an already marginalized community, Mariana is created by the directors as a compelling voice in the representation of those immigrants not considered in the intricacies of a complex (and in so much need of reformation) migratory law.

Female Empowerment Through a Boy's Gaze

The film opens with a familial scene in which Mariana is preparing empanadas for his family and friends, particularly by paying attention to her husband. Her friends are enchanted by her empanadas, but her husband seems far away and she notices it. Nevertheless, she continues smiling throughout the gathering and trying to make everyone comfortable. This initial tension develops into a fight, when Mariana's husband, Antonio, after arriving late and drunk, does not want to talk to her. In the middle of the fight, he acknowledges that he found a new job in Miami. Mariana is taken aback and it is at this moment that we learn that she and their kids, Gabriel and Andrea, just arrived in New York, after following him around all over Colombia. She allows him to leave, but she also senses that this time is different. After a few weeks of trying to reach him by phone, Mariana realizes that he abandoned her and her children.

That the crisis develops in the first ten minutes of the film is a strategy from the directors, to focus less on Mariana's victimization by her husband and instead highlight Mariana's strength and resolve to fight back. As spectators, we witness this determination through the eyes of Gabriel, her oldest child. As a ten-year-old, he is attempting to figure out their situation but also understands that his mother is trying hard to make them feel safe and happy. When Mariana and Antonio are fighting, we can see Gabriel's puzzled face, simultaneously wondering what is happening but understanding that something is not well. After his father leaves the next day, he tries to help his mother while she struggles to find some sort of job that will allow them to survive the summer. He becomes Mariana's babysitter and translator, assuming a responsibility that is beyond his age, a common situation for recent migrant children.

Two particular scenes depict Gabriel's responsibility to his family. When Mariana left him and Andrea in the apartment in order to illegally work in a restaurant washing dishes, the children became bored. A neighbor invited them to go out and they ended up having a good time in a stranger's house pool, without the homeowner's permission. There, we learned of Gabriel's hope to go to school and his wish to go to Miami to be with his father. When the owner of the house arrives, the children run away, and Gabriel hurts himself on the way back to the apartment. Mariana sees them getting on the train and desperately follows them. She is not able to get a hold of them at the moment but arrives at the apartment before they do. Gabriel tries to lie and his mother is about to punish him, but she realizes he is hurt. Gabriel is really apologetic and afraid. When Mariana thinks of taking him to the emergency room, his gaze changes into disillusionment, as his mother cannot afford to give him medical care. Again, he understands that nothing is going as planned, but he is still a kid who wants to go to school and enjoy his childhood. After this incident, Mariana realizes that Gabriel can take care of his little sister, but he is not a grown man who can act as a father.

The second scene in which Gabriel is central to the action and Mariana's decisions, comes after they start collecting cans as a way to be together and earn some money. After a long day, they arrive at their apartment and the landlord is closing the door. They cannot go in unless they pay the three months her husband Antonio owes. Mariana is confused, she does not understand, and Gabriel gives the landlord the information. She becomes desperate, as she discovers that Antonio left without paying any rent. Gabriel's eyes express this same realization and he slips into the apartment through a window to get a few of their belongings. When the landlord threatens to get the police, they run away with some clothing and the shopping cart they used for collecting cans. They end up at a park where the children begin to play and they enjoy the afternoon, while Mariana knows they do not have anywhere to go.

In order to give the spectators Gabriel's perspective of the situation, the directors are not openly directing anyone's gaze, but they meticulously use close-ups, intimately showing Gabriel's face and reactions. The actor Sebastián Villada's eyes are big and full of emotion, providing the directors with a special, important, and a subtle point of view. The music that accompanies his doings around the city, looking for small work to help his mother and to take care of his sister, complements his gestures and projection of Gabriel's feelings, allowing for the story to be more about the human experience than the political situation.

Every human experience, however, is also political and the directors work toward humanizing this family. The purpose of the simple technical construction of the film is to engage the spectators, to put themselves in Mariana's shoes while she is holding her children, on a park bench, with nowhere to go, no money, and no place to protect her kids. She is completely abandoned and homeless and Gabriel is her last ally. He depends on her to feel protected and guarded; she depends on him to manage a hostile world and the new language that is accessible to him. Gabriel becomes an active participant and witness of Mariana's story. This alliance is the first one that she can count on in order to move forward.

The Small Things Are the Big Things

Although her husband abandoned her, throughout the film Mariana demonstrates she is not a victim. She is proactive in her situation and always tries to take care of her kids the best way she can. The screenwriters and directors decided not to give Mariana a "rags to riches" story in which the

American dream is fulfilled, but a story in which the American dream is never obtained and an alternate happy ending is provided. This story is about the small things that help a woman and her family stay safe as they build a new life in a new country.

In order to survive, Mariana needed to know her community. She would go out with the kids and ask for work, look for help from strangers, and have confidence in herself. Knowing her empanadas were good, she tries to sell them in a restaurant but then confronts potential sexual harassment. She was desperate for work, but not that desperate. She decided not to accept these predatory circumstances, a decision not many immigrant women can make, because of their children. She, then, sells her empanadas on the street, looking for other work options, and she sees one when noticing how some women in a corner were picked up by another woman for different jobs. She ended up taking a few shifts washing dishes in a restaurant, but she could not leave her children alone again after the pool scene. Through these small moments, the directors are covering up many of the difficulties immigrants, especially women, go through when looking for jobs. No matter their immigrant status—undocumented or documented—the United States is a new place for them, with different dynamics and cultural codes that take some time to adapt. Mariana's non-stop motivation and positive attitude, however, demonstrate this immigrant family's resiliency.

One day, while the kids were in a movie theater—because she could only afford two tickets—she noticed an old couple collecting cans. She knows there is something there and follows an old man only to understand how the cans bring cash and she can stay with the kids. Through this new line of work, she makes a new ally, Joe, who through Gabriel's translations, helped her to understand how the process of collecting cans worked, guided her to a cheap apartment when they were homeless, and took them to a soup kitchen when they had not had much to eat. Joe is African-American, a racial ally to Mariana's brown skin and foreign accent, and someone with a resilient body who also inhabits the U.S. marginal community in a big city. He was the only one who would understand her situation and the only one capable enough to help her navigate this new marginal aspect of society in which she found herself. That the directors decided to cast Anthony Chisholm as Joe is a statement of diversity and an intentional bridge to present how both communities, the African-American and the Latinx community, can support each other in order to survive their marginal status in U.S. society.

Via Joe, Mariana also finds Preet, a third and important ally who is the landlady of the cheap apartment complex Joe recommended. She is from India and, just like Mariana, a single mother. She allows her to stay in the apartment as a favor to her and her children, but later on when Mariana finds out that she is pregnant again with Antonio's third child, a last reminder of his abandonment, Preet helps her make an important decision. She understands her friend's financial problems and struggles to give a better chance for her kids and herself and offers Mariana to perform a home abortion. After this intimate intervention in Mariana's life, Preet becomes one of her most trusted friends. Like Joe, Preet is also an ethnic ally, who is part of an underestimated and discriminated community in the United States; but furthermore, she is an ally because of her gender. She understands Mariana's needs as a Brown woman and her struggles as a mother; "I've been where you are and you will be alright," Preet told her while holding the brew she needs to drink to start the abortion process. After this situation, Preet allows her to stay and pay her rent in small payments throughout the month.

The abortion was not an easy decision for Mariana but is one that she makes in order to survive. The directors focus on the abortion scene as a hurtful and emotionally charged decision, having Mariana in the bathroom and Andrea calling for her, worried about her mom. This decision and Preet's alliance, however, allow her to achieve some stability for her family by the end of one summer.

The story of Mariana, Gabriel, and Andrea is not a story of grand stance statements, but one in which people's small, caring actions and decisions along the way help a family survive. The directors do not take big positions—as with homelessness or abortion—but present each situation as plausible, as an example of Mariana's struggles to achieve a better position in a society that does not take her life into account for being a different story. On this difference, however, there is a positionality regarding immigration, gender, and family.

Paola Mendoza and Gloria La Morte started the writing of the film to honor Paola's mother, an inspiration for the screenwriters to present a different face of immigration, one that in political struggles is always in the shadows and not taken into account when considering immigration reform. Women, mostly single mothers, are the ones holding on to their families in the United States in order to make a better life. Like Mariana, many are abandoned due to the circumstances of a patriarchal society that is always pushing men out of their domestic life and abandoning their families (either by leaving or by not paying attention to them). The gender roles in family dynamics are strict and more demanding for mothers and daughters. Mendoza and La Morte approached this conflict by focusing mostly on the determination of an immigrant mother, her openness to find allies that will help her, and, particularly, to get her strength from collaborating with her children. The interaction in these human stories is not made through a grandiloquent political gesture but by carefully observing them and portraying the big impact of small things, of small actions.

As the film title communicates, it portrays a situation "between us," something that only those with similar experiences can understand and may make meaning out of watching the film. Both directors continued their careers as filmmakers and advocates for various social issues; their most recent collaboration was on short films distributed on social media focusing on the separation of families at the border. The same intimate intensity of *Entre Nos* is continued in these films, attempting to convey a dialogue in which both sides are even in the search for justice.

As a different immigration story, *Entre Nos* is breaking Latinx stereotypes, particularly of Latina mothers. Mariana is not in need of a man to save her, nor is she a sensual vixen; she is a mother who makes mistakes and who looks for a better situation and a better life for her children and herself. Although cinematographically the film is simple, the point is to focus on the story of Mariana, of her family, and to create a counter-discourse on immigration, family, inter-ethnic alliances, gender roles, and homelessness. Mariana's situation is not one in which the directors are looking for pity, but empathy in the struggle to survive and make it better for the future of each marginalized community represented in the film.

Bibliography

"Entre Nos: Tribeca Film Institute at The New School." *YouTube*, March 2, 2010. https://youtu.be/vBoEIlcYcvQ

"Entre Nos: Interview Director Paola Mendoza, Gloria LaMorte and Liliana Legge." *YouTube*. August 1, 2009. https://youtu.be/KEfboDYBPuw

"Paola Mendoza Takes Her Immigrant Experience from the Screen to the Page." *Remezcla*, December 6, 2013, http://remezcla.com/film/paola-mendoza-takes-her-immigrant-experience-from-the-screen-to-the-page/.

"Tribeca Takes: Paola Mendoza on Entre Nos." *Tribeca*, May 15, 2018, http://remezcla.com/film/paola-mendoza-takes-her-immigrant-experience-from-the-screen-to-the-page/.

Williams, Kam. "Entre Nos Film Review." *News Blaze*. May 22, 2010, https://newsblaze.com/entertainment/movie-reviews/entre-nos-film-review_13906/.

Webster, Amy. "An Immigrant Story." *The New York Times*. May 13, 2010, https://www.nytimes.com/2010/05/14/movies/14entre.html.

Laurier, Joanne. "Entre Nos (Between Us) and *Red Father*: Aspects of US Life and History." *World Socialist Web Site*, June 23, 2014, https://www.wsws.org/en/articles/2014/06/23/film-j23.html.

Entre Nos. IMDb. https://www.imdb.com/title/tt1212456/?ref_=ttfc_fc_tt. November 13, 2018.

"Tribeca '09 Interview: 'Entre Nos' Co-directors Gloria LaMorte and Paola Mendoza." *IndieWire*, April 16, 2009, https://www.indiewire.com/2009/04/tribeca-09-interview-entre-nos-co-directors-gloria-la-morte-and-paola-mendoza-70655/.

CHAPTER 8

La Hija Natural (Dir. Leticia Tonos. 2011, República Dominicana)

Abstract Set in a rural area of the Dominican Republic, this film is not a representation of the patriarchal presence on the island, a common portrayal in many Dominican films. What Leticia Tonos achieved with this film is to delicately disarm this heteropatriarchal discourse through her character Maria. The analysis demonstrates this patriarchal disarming by describing how Tonos' direction is influenced by quotidian situations that marvelously transform her characters. Searching for her father, Maria confronts her fears and learns more about her lost mother. She becomes a woman on her own terms, creating a safe space where she is able to reconcile with her father. Manhood is questioned through humor; womanhood is developed through survival. By creating a masculine crisis and a thriving female character, Tonos is subverting the patriarchal narrative without condemning one side or the other.

Keywords Gender roles • Magical realism • Patriarchy • Feminine gaze • Masculinity • Dominican cinema

Production

Production	Línea Espiral, Isla Films, DG Cine, Ministerio de Cultura, Programa Ibermedia, Corporación de Cine de Puerto Rico, Fundación Global Democracia y Desarrollo (FUNGLODE), Instituto Global de Multimedia (IGM)
Direction	Leticia Tonos
Cinematography	Sonnel Velásquez
Producers	Leticia Tonos (producer), Zunilda Paniagua (executive producer), Frances Lausell y Sonia Fritz (executive producers)
Screenwriting	Leticia Tonos
Edition	Raúl Marchand Sánchez

Cast

María	Julietta Rodríguez
Joaquín	Víctor Checo
Polo Montifa	Gastner Legerme
Mélido	Dionis Rufino
Justiniano	Andrés Ramos
Juana	Kalent Zaiz
Rubí	Frank Perozo
Padre Contreras	Jochy Santos
Pura, la Bruja	Vickiana
El Míster	Luis Brian Mesa
La Bestia	Juan Carlos Muñoz
La Rubia	Maggy Liranzo
Doña Consuelo	Ramona Leriano
Papito	Héctor Sierra

Synopsis

María is a young woman from the countryside in the Dominican Republic who lives a quiet life with her hardworking mother, Juana. She was always intrigued by the absence of her father and dreamed of meeting him one day. Juana, however, never gave her a clue of his whereabouts. The day María loses her mother to an accident, she decides to travel and look for him. Following her neighbor's instructions, she finally arrives at her father's hometown. Joaquín, her father, is surprised by her arrival and asks his Haitian "mayordomo" (butler), Montifa, to dismiss her. Montifa convinces Joaquín to allow her to help around the house, a decision that changes their lives. It is the beginning of a journey in search of her identity and of potential redemption for Joaquín.

Director's Take: Leticia Tonos (Santo Domingo, Dominican Republic)

Leticia Tonos is the first Dominican woman to write, produce, and direct a feature film in the Dominican Republic. In an atmosphere where light and misogynistic comedies had defined the country's cinema, Tonos rises as a new voice and paradigm of a new Dominican cinematography. This new cinematography surges due to the 2010 Cinema Law 108-10, which institutionalized and nationalized the country's filmography by protecting its productions with Dominican workers and creators. *La Hija Natural [Love Child]* was developed under this context, benefitting from financial and technical support from Dirección General de Cine (DG Cine), the office created under the cinema law to apply and distribute financial information and resources to Dominican producers and directors.

Leticia Tonos' trajectory is defined by her opportunities to work on different media sources: television, advertisement, and film. She graduated with a major in advertisement from APEC (Acción Pro Educación y Cultura) University in Santo Domingo, completed her Master's degree at the Universidad Internacional in Andalucía, Spain, and finished her Film Studies at the London Film School. Her formal education weaves in her practical education, as she was part of the production of films like *Azúcar Amarga [Bitter Sugar]* (1996), *Perico Ripiao [Ripped Parrot]* (2003), and *Crisis en la Habana [Havana Crisis]* (2005). Her short-film thesis to graduate from the London Film School, *Ysrael*, based on Junot Diaz's short story, received international acclaim. Both the direction and cinematography of *Ysrael* embody Tonos' cinematic interests: themes like representation of Dominicanness, reflections on identity, and search for belonging created through long camera shots, smooth and delicately framed, emphasizing a curious perception from the protagonists.

In an interview on the program "Cultura 60" (YouTube), Tonos commented that she is interested in "cualquier tema que explore nuestra propia identidad–que tan bien nos enseña ese espejo tan grande que es el cine–cómo somos ... [any topic that may explore our identity–which is so widely shown on that big mirror that is cinema–who we are]." These are all topics that are always present in her films. *La Hija Natural* and her most recent films, *Cristo Rey* (2013) and *Mis 500 Locos* [*A State of Madness*] (2020), reflect Tonos' search to create a different cinema, distanced from the easy and superficial comedy. Her cinematic productions, unlike her previous work, have better and well-developed screenplays, Dominican characters that are in dialogue with universal discussions, and careful planning of the visual elements that are ingrained in the plot characterization.

Although she is consistently praised as the first successful female director, she brushes this admiration aside by often highlighting the work of other women in Dominican productions. She agrees, however, that there is still work to be done to acknowledge the filmographic work of women, especially regarding executive decisions. In the same "Cultura 360" interview, she comments that, sometimes, it is women who also influence their lack of visibility by being too careful about how they navigate the industry, which transpires an ambiguity in Tonos' approach to a feminist perspective. Nevertheless, her colleague and director from *Perico Ripiao*, Ángel Muñiz, stresses that *La Hija Natural* is a film only a woman "could manage" ["podía manejar"] (*La Hija Natural*, "Detrás de cámara." YouTube). Without a condescending or paternalistic tone, Muñiz represents Tonos' filmographic approach as a reflection and a refreshing perspective of fundamental Dominican topics and, at the same time, considerations about the state of women in developing countries. Tonos does not identify herself as a feminist but prefers to integrate herself into the new route Dominican cinema is taking, both by being the founder of ADOCINE and president of her own production company Línea Espiral. Her cinematic and thematic approaches redefine, under her feminist gaze, the filmographic and previous producing discourses in the Dominican Republic.

COMMENTARY AND CONTEXT

The Dominican film industry gained momentum after the approval of the Film Law 108-10, as it was affirmed by its most passionate defender, Ellis Pérez, DGCine director. The law was approved in 2010 and its objective is "propiciar un desarrollo progresivo, armónico y equitativo de la cinematografía nacional y, en general, promover la actividad cinematográfica en la República Dominicana [to promote a progressive, harmonic and equal development of the national cinematography and, in general, to promote the cinematographic activity in the Dominican Republic]" (Ley 108-10). This support would come from private financial investment, which would be coordinating with the government the distribution of this backing in a systemic, organized, and fair way. Producers, actors, and investors supported this legislation with the aim of expanding film production on the island beyond light comedies and films with superficial plots. As Tonos commented in an interview with *15 minutos* (YouTube), "la comedia es importante, pero es importante desarrollarnos de otra manera [comedy is important, but is also important to develop ourselves in other ways]." This development started with the investors, who financially supported comedy projects that guaranteed a large audience and large profits, while other more complex film initiatives did not reach a pre-production status. Under the new law, private investment is protected, as it is subsidized by state income taxes. Thus, both producers and investors win: the producers receive the money to complete their project, and the investors will recover their money if ticket sales do not yield a profit.

The production of *La Hija Natural* started when these legislative changes were still developing. Tonos, however, as director and producer, received the support of the recently created DGCine to complete the final stages of production. Besides having the financial support needed, Tonos also played with the audience's expectations by including in the cast well-known Dominican celebrities, such as a show-host and vedette Vickiana and the comedian Jochy Santos. This balance between securing financial support and cast decisions helped Tonos stir up curiosity in the spectators about her project, with promotional interviews. In addition, the topic of a "hija natural" [love child], not recognized by her father, is common in the Dominican experience. As some spectators reacted and commented after the film premiere, it is a situation with which they can identify ("Premiere La Hija Natural," YouTube). This identification of Tonos' view with the audience went beyond expectations by being the Dominican pick to the Academy of Motion Picture Arts and Sciences for consideration for the Oscar as Best Foreign Film. *La Hija Natural* became a semi-finalist, and although it did not make it to the final list, it was a win for Dominican film, a recognition that had not happened since 1995 with *Nueba Yol*. This success spoke of Leticia Tonos' careful craftsmanship in her filmographic aesthetic and vision.

Her attention to visual cinematography is Tonos' main character as a director. *Variety* magazine stated that "visually, the pic is unfailingly attractive," especially in the color selections, which determines the characters' representations. Greens, blues, and earth tones help to the construction of the rural atmosphere and also speak of its characters: María, the protagonist, wears the festive colors of the rural landscape, while her father,

Joaquín, limits his palette with colors representing the land—yellow and soft browns—as is the land that he works and defends from Mélido, his brother in law. In the same way, María is joyful, and positive, while Joaquín is taciturn, and melancholic at times.

Although Tonos is focused on the relationships and identity search of a daughter, the film is not ambitious in its feminist projection or, at least, in its discussion about Dominican women's position in society. María is able to come out of her comfort zone and look for an adventure in order to find her father, who had never recognized or met her, but Joaquín is not punished for his arrogance toward women: "Because Tonos has based her film on observation of how things are rather than on propaganda about how they should be, audiences seeking a feminist message may find the pic's upbeat conclusion a little too forgiving of Joaquín's dreadful sexism" (Variety, n.p.). Nevertheless, through her visualization and crafting of her original screenplay, Tonos is able to question gender relationships, especially in the Dominican Republic where heteronormative gender relations are mostly traditional.

The characters in the film are not allegories of Dominicanness but personalities that are dealing with daily life and, occasionally, with the fantastic. They live in the countryside, navigating its beauty, which is a different take on the Dominican Republic, as it is set up outside of the urban capital, Santo Domingo, exploring the construction of a dysfunctional family away from the city. The film is not positioned to define Dominicanness but is installed inside this identity in order to present a picture that may speak about this national identity without defining it. María is a typical young woman, living with her mother, going to school, watching telenovelas, and sharing her life with her neighbors. Joaquín is also a typical macho, but in his widowhood was left completely vulnerable and almost uprooted from his property, as it was his wife's, who had legitimate ownership of the land. That vulnerability in a crisis is what Tonos explores in this film, taking the spectators on a journey of subtle emotions and ludic mysteries inside these personal relationships.

"Alejandra, yo soy tu padre [I Am Your Father]": The Telenovela as a Referential Framework

La Hija Natural is the story of María's sentimental education in a rural area of the Dominican Republic. This education profoundly depends on the conventional heteronormative gender roles that dominate this society and that Tonos depicts from the beginning of her film. After a brief prologue in which we see María as a girl, the second time that we see her she is a young woman, on her neighbor's balcony, watching a telenovela with other neighbors. The telenovela's title correlates with the film's, *La Hija Natural*, providing a clue of the film's framework: on the one hand, the theme of a daughter's search for her father; on the other, the gender roles that define this search.

Intrigued, escaping the heat of the night and the community, María and her neighbors learned who the telenovela protagonist's father is. The protagonist's name is "María Alejandra," a clear connection to the film's protagonist. The camera close-up on María's face shows us all her reactions, curiosity, preoccupation, and calmness, while the telenovela protagonist accepts the apologies from her father through a chivalrous act: he gives her his handkerchief to dry her tears. When father and daughter embrace in the telenovela, María smiles, emotionally affected because as a "hija natural" [love child] herself, she also dreams of meeting her father. Her reality is completely different from the telenovelas, but this does not stop her curiosity about her father and her hope to meet him. She asked her mother: "¿Usted cree que vuelva? Doña Consu dice que él no vive lejos de aquí [Do you think he might come back? Mrs. Consu says that he does not live far from here]," her mother calmly answered, "Ay, mija, la mujer que le cree a un hombre está perdía. Usted me tiene que prometer que no va a ser tan blandita como yo [Oh, daughter, the woman that trusts a man is lost. You need to promise me that you will not be soft, like I was]," an answer to which María reacts with skepticism.

The protagonist's sentimental education is defined, thereby, by the traditional gender roles she watched in the telenovelas, which respond to a standard family perspective. In the telenovelas, family is disarticulated via the dramatic chaos of its characters, to later re-articulate it back to its traditional form—a mother, and a father figure with a child as their reason and future—without any difficulty, all together through chance and *deux ex machina*. Additionally, the moral discourse that is constructed in the telenovelas responds to the patriarchal discourse; it upholds the male protagonist as the agent to resolve, in the end, the tragedy of the female protagonist who is usually a damsel in distress, with no money and no family. Nonetheless, Juana, María's mother, shows her that men in general, especially her father, are not to be trusted. In the film, this family is kept disarticulated, with no clear indication of how the tragedy would be solved and is not completely guided by patriarchal standards. María needs to be strong and she must create her own destiny, break the traditional gender molds, and find her father on her own terms.

By questioning the telenovela discourse, Leticia Tonos affirms the need for a new space for María, the love child of the film we are watching. This new space is on the limits of patriarchy, out of the paternalistic influence—both on the discursive and the filial—as María grew up without her father, distanced from his influence and his example. Although she dreams of meeting him, her mother's and her own actions are not defined by his absence but by their own survival. Juana works two jobs so María can continue her studies, and María responds with good behavior, support, and love. Their mother-daughter relationship is profound and without melodrama. Nevertheless, dramatic events follow the protagonist.

Contrary to the telenovela narrative, María is not abandoned, but her mother dies in an accident. Their house is situated at the edge of a road through which trucks pass speeding by. While María is at school one day, a speeding truck drives off the road, destroys the house, and kills Juana. María is not able to say goodbye, as the ambulance takes her mother before she gets home. Now practically an orphan, she decides to look for her father.

When María meets Joaquín and begins a relationship with him, this narrative does not follow the telenovela dramatic conventions either. A series of dialogues and awkward and strange encounters begin to construct a relationship, distancing rather than getting María closer to Joaquín. It is not until a young man, Justiniano, arrives in town and threatens María's security that her father demonstrates any paternal sensibility toward her. At that moment he is able to defend María's honor (and his as well) and to hold the young man accountable for his actions against his daughter, claiming a responsibility that he never demonstrated while having affairs with women other than her mother. When everything is solved with Justiniano, however, María decides to leave Joaquín's house.

When she leaves and breaks with the passive role of the patient woman that telenovelas ascribed to her, Joaquín realizes his mistake and goes to look for her. At the bus station, while she is waiting for the bus to leave town, Joaquín finds her and the two of them talk about the scars they had from their relationship with Juana (when angry, she used to throw things at whoever was in a fight with her), and from this intimate moment, something akin to father-daughter relationship begins to develop. Nevertheless, María is not completely convinced. After a small silence, she says to him: "Ella se murió esperándolo [she died waiting for you]," bringing up his abandonment, to what Joaquín answers, "Yo sé que no hice gran cosa para reparar eso, pero tú viniste por mí [I know I did not do enough to repair that, but you came to look for me]," bringing up both María's vulnerability as well as her agency. His daughter did not need to wait for him. She searched for him and found him. María, by being strong, as her mother made her promise (to not be soft), was able to bring Joaquín close to her; by being the agent of her own destiny, she begins to empower herself. She cries a little and Joaquín, parallel to the telenovela, offers her his handkerchief to dry her tears. She takes it, but the climatic and dramatic hug does not happen. There is still a long way for them to become father and daughter, and she is not "soft," keeping her promise to her mother. The gender roles framed in the telenovela are exposed and the patriarchal discourse that is contained in it is questioned.

Gender Roles and the Supernatural

In a comedic and magical way, Leticia Tonos questions Dominican gender roles without using strong or overtly feminist strategies. Laughter, parody, and magical realism are her subtle tools to disarticulate the patriarchal discourse that has strongly influenced the country's history and society. These strategies are illustrated in two scenes related to María's vulnerability after her mother died and when she is trying to figure out her relationship with Joaquín. Doña Consu helps María overcome the loss of her mother by allowing her to stay in her house for as long as she needs. Papito, Doña Consu's husband, is the typical "man of the house," who goes out to work but does not help with any domestic chores. After agreeing to let María stay for a while, Papito looks at her with desire, which prompts María to always be getting away from him. At one point when both Doña Consu and María were washing dishes and talking, Papito wanted to impose his authority. He ordered Doña Consu to find him his pants. When she answered that the pants were dirty, he went out of the room, and while he was not there, Doña Consu commented to María that she had pawned the pants and knew it would be a challenge to avoid Papito's anger. When Papito returned, he was enraged and was screaming for his pants again. To emphasize his demand he took a small vase and threw it to the floor.

The director's good humor and comedic perspective are demonstrated at this particular moment. The vase, instead of breaking, bounced back, and Papito was dumbfounded. The vase was not made of glass, as he thought, but plastic. Calmly, Doña Consu responded to this action, without laughing but with a triumphant look, by saying that in her house she did not have any glass decorations anymore because he was always breaking them. At this point, she left the room and came back with another pair of pants. This is a comic scene from the spectator's point of view because here, without any drama, two macho conventions are confronted: violence and women's submission. On the one hand, Doña Consu negotiates the apparent submission by not letting Papito know that she pawned his pants—which also demonstrates her skills of self-sufficiency—and that she replaced all her glass decorations with plastic. Her experiences with her volatile husband allowed her to become more audacious instead of fearful, therefore, challenging Dominican patriarchy. On the other hand, Papito's machismo is undermined by Doña Consu's audacity, disarming it completely and revealing the infantile manner of his capricious authority. Papito tries to recover his authority by sexually harassing María, but she is able to get away from him. At that moment, she knows that she is alone and vulnerable and must look for her father.

In this film, the new space of feminine representation is based on two conventional discourses about women: nature and the supernatural. Nature is represented throughout the film via the presence of a ladybug, a symbol traditionally related to good luck. The supernatural happens at the end of the film, with a scene that also involves ladybugs but in a magical realist setting. Just like she does with the representations of masculinity, Tonos is able to disarm feminine conventions but without confronting them directly.

Ladybugs are related to María's character, who is always looking for them. At the beginning of the film, in a scene that serves as a brief prologue to her and her mother, we see María as a child. Is early in the morning and she is looking for ladybugs when, from afar, a truck is getting dangerously near the road where María is. Juana is able to get her before something bad happens to her and claims "¿Cuántas veces te he dicho que no comas esos bichos raros [how many times have I told you not to eat those strange bugs]?" to which María responds by crying. Instead of a good luck symbol, the ladybug serves as a potential bad omen. Anytime María finds them or eats them, something goes wrong. For example, right before we learn about Juana's death, María is at school, watching a baseball match, when she feels a ladybug crawling on her leg. Without thinking, she eats it. In the next scene, she is walking home and, from a distance, sees her house in ruins and learns about Juana's death and her life changes forever. It could be argued, however, that María violates this clear symbolic aspect of the ladybug, as a good or bad omen. According to popular belief, a ladybug is good luck if it is walking or flying, but it brings bad luck if it is killed. María does not kill them, but instead, she eats them, feeding from them, as if eating and absorbing their good luck. The symbol, then, is not undoubtedly defined but ambiguous.

The ambiguity of the ladybugs is solved at the end of the film. It begins in the scenes when María feels that she has been betrayed by her boyfriend, Justiniano, when she believes they might be having an incestuous relationship as he is also looking for his father. María feels that Joaquín has also abandoned her again. While she was walking in the plaza, she noticed the San Juan festivities and the nightly ceremony when everybody offered a light—a candle—to the saint. María's light is from Pura, the town's witch, whom she met previously for a spiritual consultation. When María started to live in Joaquín's house, she witnessed strange things around it. With Montifa, the butler, María went to Pura's house to understand why these events—an empty, rocking chair moving, rotten eggs—were occurring. During that first consultation, Pura told her: "El hambre te hacía comer mariquitas. Las tienes todas revoloteando dentro de ti. Hasta que no veas las cosas con tus propios ojos y no con los de tu madre, no lo sabrás [Hunger led you to eat ladybugs. They are all fluttering inside you. Until you see things with your own eyes and not with your mother's, you will never know]." After Pura and María meet again in the plaza, she becomes her spiritual guide and offers her solutions to her spiritual discomfort.

María returns home with Pura, but Joaquín is not there, only Montifa. She changed her clothing, now wearing a red dress that belonged to her mother and while carrying a candle, the three of them went into the banana plantation, the place from where all the strange things were coming. Each took a different path, Montifa went left, Pura to the right—but staying close to María—and María walked toward the center. While they searched for what was causing a curse in the house, María saw a ladybug walking on a plantain leaf. She does not eat it but contemplates it and smiles. Immediately, she began to feel sick and placed a hand on her stomach, as if it were hurting. From the back of the plantation, Mélido, Joaquín's brother-in-law, who is fighting for part of the land that his sister left to Joaquín, appeared near María. He was drunk and confused, and in his confusion, he mistook María for Emilia, his dead sister and Joaquín's wife. Scared, Mélido asked Emilia/María why she was there. Shortly after this, María opens her mouth and all the ladybugs she had eaten throughout her life came out flying as if leaving her to make space to receive the spirit of her aunt Emilia. Emilia's ghost possessed her and responded to Mélido's question.

Through Emilia's possession, María begins to understand his vulnerabilities: he was loyal to Emilia—who was not able to bear children and knew about Joaquín's affairs, that he was completely unfaithful to the other women who gave him offsprings. Joaquín's weakness was not being able to get over his wife's death, to embrace his widowhood in order to change and make peace with his past. Through these scenes, gender roles and traditional social conventions on gender are exposed but not completely transformed. Joaquín and Emilia are guided by a patriarchal system, but their relationship and attitude toward marriage break away from the traditional discourse to leave them wide open and vulnerable, creating a small opportunity for other alternatives. Similarly, the ladybugs, symbols of nature and an ambiguous good fortune are María's alternative link to knowledge of herself and of her new life.

Knowledge comes from the afterlife, in the kingdom of the deceased women, who are the ones to define the path of María and Joaquín's relationship. Emilia, Joaquín's wife, becomes the mediator of Joaquín's economic stability, dismissing Mélido's demands, so Joaquín can begin his life anew by working the land she left him, and feel like a hardworking man again. Likewise, Juana, María's mom, is the echo that, in Joaquín's dreams, constantly reminds him of his debt, his lack of loyalty toward María, and that he needed to acknowledge her as his daughter. From the afterlife, Emilia and Juana are the matriarchal voices that open a space for María to reconcile with Joaquín, but in her own terms, outside of the patriarchal influence and in a new space that, although gloomy, is an alternative to belonging and to be Joaquín's daughter. As the director of these stories and spaces, Leticia Tonos is strategically feminist, uncovering the gaps in the patriarchal discourse and offering María a third space to reconstruct her life in harmony, remembering her mother and regaining hope for her father to become a better man.

Bibliografía

"15 minutos con Leticia Tonos y Pamela Sued en Sigue la Noche." *YouTube*, December 12, 2013. https://www.youtube.com/watch?v=Na81AKluTLQ

"Capítulo 16. Leticia Tonos." *Cultura 360*, YouTube. February 28, 2013, https://www.youtube.com/watch?v=6ZickLwuhbI

"La hija natural. Detrás de cámara." *YouTube*. February 21, 2011, https://www.youtube.com/watch?v=7cwe752IUx4

"Premiere, La hija natural." *YouTube*, March 31, 2011, https://www.youtube.com/watch?v=ahyFIDgh82Y

"Resumen Ejecutivo sobre la Ley No. 108-10 para el Fomento de la Actividad Cinematográfica en la República Dominicana y su Reglamento por Decreto No. 370-11." *DMK Lawyer*, http://www.dmklawyers.com/ES/publicaciones/203-resumen-ejecutivo-sobre-la-ley-no-108-10-para-el-fomento-de-la-actividad-cinematografica-en-la-republica-dominicana-y-su-reglamento-por-decreto-no-370-11.html

Holland, Jonathan. "Review: Love Child." *Variety*, December 6, 2011, http://variety.com/2011/film/reviews/love-child-1117946703/

PART IV

Depatriarchalizing

CHAPTER 9

Mosquita y Mari (Aurora Guerrero. 2012, USA)

Abstract This film by Aurora Guerrero focuses on the relationship and friendship of two young Chicanas: Yolanda (Mosquita) and Mari. As a traditional coming-of-age story, the film follows the young women, their struggles in school, with friends, and, particularly, their struggles with their parents, while they start relying on each other a little more intimately as they become best friends. Although the film does not conclude with a coming-out story, Yolanda's exploration of new opportunities via her friendship with Mari expands through the director's queer gaze. Their relationship is treated not as an anomaly, as heteronormative conventions try to define the LGBTQ+ experience, but as part of discovering oneself. This intimacy between Yolanda and Mari is analyzed through the perspective of a coming-of-age story in a Latinx community with its specific cultural expectations and education—particularly for the studious Yolanda; the impact of family on the decisions these young women (and any Latina) must confront in order to be successful; and how identity and sexuality are interrelated with the cultural expectations and family influence on self-discovery and a potential future. Guerrero does not offer a strong political statement, but a quotidian, tender gaze on these young Chicanas and how they learn to navigate the complex community in which they live.

Keywords Coming of age • Lesbians • Friendship • Family • Latinas • Latino film

Production

Production	Indion Entertainment Group/Mayan Entertainment Group
Director	Aurora Guerrero
Producers	Chad Burris, Jim Mckay
Screenwriter	Aurora Guerrero
Director of Photography	Magela Crosignani
Editing	Augie Robles

Cast

Yolanda "Mosquita"	Fenessa Pineda
Mari	Venecia Troncoso
Mr. Olveros	Joaquin Garrido
Mrs. Olveros	Laura Patalano
Mrs. Rodriguez	Dulce Maria Solis
Vicky	Marisela Uscanga
Vero	Melissa Uscanga

Synopsis

The film focuses on a friendship between two young Chicanas growing up in Huntington Park, California. As part of immigrant families, both girls are expected to take advantage of their parent's sacrifices. Yolanda is shy and studious, while Mari needs to help her mother with economic responsibilities while studying. An incident at school leads them to begin a friendship that allows them to discover themselves and develop their identities. As their attraction for one another grows, they explore their relationship and subtle sexual desires (Fig. 9.1).

Director's Take: Aurora Guerrero (California, the United States)

A queer Chicana writer and director, Aurora Guerrero uses the camera as a way to promote social change. She was born in San Francisco, California, and raised in the Bay Area. Her parents migrated from Veracruz, Mexico, and she witnessed their financial struggles in their family business. Her participation in youth leadership programs in San Francisco enabled her to learn about the power of the arts and how they can be used to promote

Fig. 9.1 *Mari y Mosquita* bonding

empowerment in the Latinx community. From these experiences, she was inspired to use film as a means to educate, heal, and promote social change.

Guerrero began her filmmaking career late in her life. She graduated with a BA in Psychology and Chicano Studies at UC Berkeley and completed her Master of Fine Arts at California Institute of the Arts in Santa Clarita. In 2005, she was selected as a Sundance Institute-Ford Foundation film fellow. During this fellowship, she participated in the Native Indigenous Lab with the *Mosquita y Mari* (*MyM*) script. In 2012, this script became Guerrero's first feature film, which debuted at the Sundance Film Festival, a first for a Chicana filmmaker that was also a Sundance Institute and Ford Foundation Fellow. Before *Mosquita y Mari*, she participated as an assistant director to the productions by Patricia Cardoso and Peter Bratt, *Real Women Have Curves* (2002) and *La Mission* (2009), respectively. After *Mosquita y Mari* she has been very active in directing several series such as *Queen Sugar* (2016), *Cherish in the Day* (2020), *Gentefied* (2020), *Little America* (2020), *13 Reasons Why* (2017–2020), among others. Her active participation in mainstream and alternative TV is remarkable in an era where streamed series produce and administer most of the cultural meaning in U.S. society.

Commentary and Context

The story of *Mosquita y Mari* is connected to Guerrero's coming of age, as it is inspired by her own personal experiences. Instead of creating a biopic, however, she wanted to make a film that would illustrate the coming of age of two young Chicanas and their sexual exploration. Instead of portraying a story of two female adolescents falling in love, she complicates the narrative and the depiction of their sexual attraction and the gendered discourses that surround the protagonists in relation to the social expectations of gender and sexuality. In this sense, Guerrero is adopting a queer point of view, challenging the dynamics that establish compulsory heterosexuality as a sociocultural expectation in Western societies.

The location of this film is not in the Mission, San Francisco, where Guerrero was born and raised, but rather in Huntington Park, Los Angeles. In an interview, she explained that it was too difficult to film *Mosquita y Mari* in the Mission, because of the cost due to the gentrification that this area has experienced in the last 20 years. The Huntington Park area, on the other hand, gave her the geographic emotions that she was looking for in the film. The location is an industrial area, originally an Anglo community, containing many factories and made up of a large number of working-class Latinx residents. By the mid-1990s, as many members of the Anglo community moved out to the suburbs, the area became mostly populated by immigrants of Mexican descent who have been historically neglected. The actual filming of *Mosquita y Mari* was, by itself, empowering to the community. Guerrero not only used non-professional actors for her film, the two protagonists are from the area, but she maintained a connection with the community that goes beyond *Mosquita y Mari*.

In the film, the characters are divided by a generational gap. On the one hand, the parents represent the Mexican immigrant community, that first generation that needed to adapt to a new situation to better their lives and overcome the discrimination in many aspects of their lives. On the other hand, the protagonists represent a U.S. Latinx identity, as they are the second generation that is in between their Mexican inheritance, their parents' values and hopes, and what they individually want as part of U.S. society. As the film cleverly depicts, however, the pressure on both groups, the first and second generation, is high. Both protagonists have different responsibilities: Yolanda needs to devote all her time to the one thing her parents deem most important, her education; Mari spends the majority of her time working to help her mother and support her family, as it is common in many Latinx house-holds (Skogrand and Hatch 2005).

Mosquita y Mari has a singular approach to the discussion and representation of sexuality and affectivity. The term "Mosquita" comes from "mosquita muerta" (a fly playing dead before it flies away) and it is the term that Mari gives to the shy Yolanda. The film never explicitly addresses queer sexuality and homophobia, but the latter is implied in how the main and secondary characters react to Yolanda and Mari's friendship. They do not talk about these topics, but from their gestures, comments, or clear avoidance it can be understood that queer identities are not acceptable. The two young protagonists grow close to each other. Some scenes illustrate this closeness and their mutual, romantic feelings, but it is a relationship they do not know how to articulate between themselves or to their parents. One of the most interesting aspects of the film is this inability to articulate their relationship. Guerrero creates a history, visually and through dialogue, that is able to depict the moment in which the two adolescents begin to question their mutual emotions, affectivity, and sexual desires. In the film, it is something real for the main characters, in touch, space, and time, but not part of a direct dialogue. When Yolanda and Mari become distracted because they are spending a lot of time together, their parents' first impression is that their daughters are being distracted by boys, although later is implied in their reaction that they understand it is the girls' special friendship that is affecting Yolanda's grades. The protagonists feel comfortable with each other. The young women know, however, that their actions and feelings are not accepted by their friends, families, and, in general, the Latinx culture that surrounds them. They know not to talk about their feelings with their parents. They do not even discuss them with each other. In some sense, as Inmaculada Pertusa and Torres (2003) argue, in the Latinx cultural production from the United States, Latin America, or even in Spain, there is a common motif of silencing the pronunciation of the lesbian/queer affective dynamics and desire. The easy reflection would be that Guerrero is following that approach. This production, however, takes a sophisticated perspective that makes the poetic tone of the film into a serious analysis of the Latinx community's working context in relation to affectivity and queer identity in two young women. The silence on lesbianism is not broken by a grand statement of Mari and Mosquita's relationship but by the affection they demonstrate in the small things, in their closeness both physical and psychological. They are not able to articulate it in words but by being physically and emotionally present with each other.

The story presented by *MyM* is not the traditional coming-of-age story as it specifically focuses on Chicanas growing up in a Los Angeles, Latinx community. Both the community and family values are part of this coming of age and affect any aspect of the life of these Latinas. More than a coming of age, it is a negotiation of their individuality as potential adults and their filial responsibilities and collective commitments. It is a universal topic from the perspective of two young women, with specific backgrounds and historical struggles. These realities, from Aurora Guererro's perspective, are worth telling, as they bring up a conversation about the specificities of a community, generational changes, and gender and sexuality discussions that are mostly needed.

Coming of Age as Chicanas: Everyday Life

One of the purposes of the film is to depict the everyday life of the two main characters, Yolanda/Mosquita and Mari. Guerrero wanted to capture an experience of life and she does just that with this complex friendship. Their relationship is an escape from their reality and their stressful lives. They have a chance to explore outside the plans that, literally and metaphorically, their parents have in mind for them. The film presents a relatable story of two friends who are enjoying their time as teenagers. They go everywhere together, do everything together, and teach each other about their own lives. Yolanda/Mosquita tutors Mari in math and Mari helps her develop her individuality and courage.

The camera movement and music in one particular montage capture the reality of their friendship. At the beginning of this scene, cross-cutting, the camera follows the two protagonists from behind as they walk down the hallway at school and down the street. During this parallel editing, the girls are the only figures in focus. This parallels the idea that their lives, what they are expected to do, and most importantly, their growing friendship are at the center of everything. Nothing else around them really matters. Not only is the setting different between the parallel cuts but also how they interact with each other. As they walk down the hallway, they are more physically engaged. They touch each other and hug. When they are walking down the boulevard, however, they are not as close, but instead, they are connected through music. Mari introduces Mosquita to her music. They are constantly sharing the earphones of a CD player that Mari owns. Mosquita is a shy girl who usually follows her strict routine which consists of school and homework. When she meets Mari, her routine begins to change. Music becomes her outlet for escape, as it is Mari's.

The song that plays during this montage scene is directly related to the girls' want for escape, while still having their desire for success in mind. The song, *El Día Previo*, by Algodón Egipcio, describes someone who has been living their life and is ready for more. The lyrics resonate with the coming-of-age story. Mosquita and Mari walk all around the neighborhood and explore, both the streets and each other, just as the song mentions, "Devoré todo el pasto de esta ciudad [I devoured all the grass in this city]." They do all that they do, ready for what is next, while staying grounded, with each other and with their families, like the song says, "no me perderé [I will not get lost]." The lyrics also imply that tomorrow they could be doing something else, instead of following the social script that prevents young Chicanas from finding their own voice or identity: "Dibujé mapas en mis pies, no me perderé/Mañana llega ese nuevo chance que me inventé [I drew maps on my feet, I will not get lost/tomorrow that chance I invented, will arrive]."

Throughout this montage, the exclusion of labels is significant and is followed in the story of *Mosquita y Mari*, as the coming-of-age experience should allow for free exploration and avoiding any labeling. This exploration is significant because it subtly challenges societal norms. Patriarchal society demands labels on how one performs sexuality (straight or queer) and one's gender (male or female). Guerrero decides to not label the relationship as queer or label the girls as lesbians but prefers to represent just an ordinary bond between them as daughters, students, friends, and possible girlfriends. This matter is important in the world of the film as it captures the girls' experiences and emotions in a much more worthy focus than the open challenges the issue of sexuality and queerness may bring to the Latinx family and community. The subtlety of their relationship and bonding (Is it romantic? Is it just friendly exploration?) opens up the possibility of a dialogue on these dwelling questions about gender and sexuality that are more important out of the young women's relationship than on its development inside the film. *MyM* becomes, then, a type of exposition and documentation for a broader discussion.

Family Resistance and Self-discovery

After Yolanda's (Mosquita's) parents are aware of some distractions that are affecting her grades in school, they remind her of the importance of their family sacrifices and her expected success. This scene is of significance because as viewers, we get a sense of the different types of Latinx families the director wants to portray. Both Mosquita and Mari are from immigrant families living in the United States, and their parents are working hard to do what they must for their children to have a better life. Yolanda's parents are both present in her life, while Mari only has her mother who has to work all day long, as her father passed away when she was younger. Mosquita's parents support her and push her to succeed in her education, expecting her not to "lose sight" of her goals. On the other hand, Mari has to focus on helping her mother and sister to survive.

This scene presents a one-sided conversation that Mosquita's parents have with her in the car right after their conference with her teacher, subtly reminding her not to forget what is expected of her. They remind the audience of their sacrifices in order for her to devote her time entirely to studying. While in the car, they illustrate to Yolanda what their sacrifices mean, as they pass by sections of their own community that are in a worse financial situation than they are. In a certain way, throughout their speech and Yolanda's perspective *from* the car, she recognizes her own privilege. At this moment, the film evokes Adriene Rich's reflection about the "politics of identity": if it were a different person, a different body, she could experience life under very different circumstances; one of poverty and even more disenfranchisement. Also, *inside* the car, they are able to contain Yolanda's freedom and bring her back to how they see (and how she should see) the world, reminding her to keep her perspective on her education.

This conversation concerns an argument that the parents are making: work hard to have a better life. The visuals outside serve as supporting reasoning for making better choices. The scene opens with visuals of the homeless population, which the father says is like what they left behind in Mexico. Although this scene is happening only a few blocks from their home, her parents protect her from it and from other difficulties that she could have faced if they had been living in Mexico. The car serves as a protective "bubble," as they shield Mosquita from the dangers of their barrio. She is safe inside the car, just as she is safe inside their house. At this moment they feel like their daughter does not see the importance of their actions and words and they are scared, while Mosquita wants to enjoy her time and still make her family proud. Mosquita responds by saying she knows that her future is important, but her father gives her a hard time, wanting her to work harder. Although she understands, her body language during the car ride does not convey it; she is not fully present. She is looking out of the car window and not toward her parents in an engaged manner. She seems to be thinking and reflecting, but not so much on the conversation at hand. She is conflicted. As a young Chicana, she knows what her parents want, but she wants to think about her life at the moment and enjoy her time as a teenager.

This specific scene demonstrates how the film represents the conflictive influence of family, specifically the experiences and sacrifices of an immigrant Mexican family, as an important value of the Latinx community. Family is rooted in all that the girls do, which makes decision-making, relationships, and hopes for the future difficult at times. Coming from a Latinx background, the girls expect to live up to these sacrifices, work harder, and keep everything in focus for a better life than what their parents have, especially in the case of Mosquita. They carry the weight of the future that their parents expect from them and the challenges that come with doing what they need to do; these hopes and dreams are what bring the protagonists together.

These expectations open, then, the opportunity for the subtle exploration of their sexuality. In the film, this exploration speaks to the identities that the protagonists try to form while opening up the discussion to the homophobic attitudes (even self-internalized) of the Latinx community. After spending countless hours together, Mosquita and Mari are alone together in one scene, with the parents out of the house. This time they try something that they have not done before. As Mosquita naps, Mari lays down right beside her under the blanket. When she awakens, Yolanda begins to run her fingers along Mari's bare stomach. Homoerotic desires are never explicit in the dialogue, but instead, all actions are presented as a process of identity exploration and self-discovery. Their relationship is significant because with each other they can talk about anything and they can, apparently, express their true selves. Mosquita and Mari provide an emotional connection for each other that their parents do not. This entire scene occurs in complete silence from both characters. In the middle of the exploration of their physical connection, Mosquita's parents return, interrupting the scene.

When the parents are home, the young women act as if nothing happened and they look frightened by the fact that they could have been caught. Nothing is ever said out loud about this encounter, always the big elephant in the room. These families do not talk about sexuality or alternative queer identities that are not part of the Latinx community. When the parents, especially Yolanda's, notice their daughters are acting differently, they automatically assume that a boy is part of the problem. They cannot imagine the idea of their daughters possibly being distracted by each other, which sends a message to their children. They see that their parents have heterosexuality as a "must" and shy away from talking with them or between them about relationships. In this sense, and despite portraying again the historic silence of queer or lesbian's stories, Guerrero is challenging the discourses that give "coherence" to compulsory heterosexuality. She is not only depicting the initial desire but also connecting it to the location of these young characters: their affection, their economic and class struggles, the position of their parents on the social scale, and their situation as students, among other concerns.

Yolanda and Mari's relationship becomes strong, as they help each other grow and shape their identity. In this exploratory scene, the camera movement and the use of silence in the film convey the feelings that they have for each other. Close-up shots are used to show the actions of hands, as Mari touches Mosquita's face and Mosquita touches Mari's stomach. The close-ups allow us to see the delicate movements of the hands as they touch each other's female bodies. Traditionally, in cinema, this type of interaction is performed between a man and woman, having a scopic male perspective, but that is not the case here. Through the exchange between close-ups and medium shots that show the faces of the characters, Guerrero reminds us that the body being touched is female and that the one doing the touching is also a female character. They do not look at each other and instead are silent. They may not understand the feelings that they have for each other, but they acknowledge them with this intimacy. The absence of music opens a time for reflection as they try to understand their feelings and sensations. This reflection is noteworthy. They know that they should not be engaging in what is happening in this scene, but they are comfortable with it. On the other hand, this scene challenges the audience as the characters' actions and feelings oppose the heteronormative assumptions of a filmic relationship between two people.

By the end of the film, this emotional-sexual relationship does not evolve. A moment of betrayal forces Mosquita and Mari to take some time apart. They see each other afterward and smile at one another, communicating that they still have a strong relationship. While walking parallel to one another, Mosquita on one side of the street and Mari on the other, they acknowledge the importance of what had happened up to then and that, maybe, they will find each other at the end of their new journeys. The film provides an open ending for the friendship and for the audience to decide what the future holds for these young Chicana women.

BIBLIOGRAPHY

"Between Two Worlds: How Young Latinos Come of Age in America." *Pew Research Center*, Hispanic Trends, 2009, https://www.pewresearch.org/hispanic/2009/12/11/between-two-worlds-how-young-latinos-come-of-age-in-america/.

Erazo, Vanessa. (2013). "Aurora Guerrero on Making Mosquita y Mari & Challenging Hollywood's Lack of Diverse Stories." *Huffpost Latino Voices*, https://www.huffpost.com/entry/aurora-guerrero-on-making_b_3226548.

Erazo, Vanessa. (2014). "Aurora Guerrero on Making of Mosquita y Mari and Scouring Remezcla For New Music." *Remezcla*, https://remezcla.com/film/aurora-guerrero-mosquita-y-mari-interview/.

Fuchs, Ellise. (2012). "Most of Us Don't Need to Put Labels on It: An Interview with Aurora Guerrero." *Popmatters*, https://www.popmatters.com/164954-interview-with-aurora-guerrero-2495801265.html.

Guerrero, Aurora. (2011). "Kick It: Aurora Guerrero Finds Strength in Relationships." *Sundance Institute*, https://www.sundance.org/blogs/creative-distribution-initiative/kick-it-aurora-guerrero-finds-strength-in-relationships/.

Hidalgo, Alexandra. (2015). "Aurora Guerrero." *Agnesfilms*, https://agnesfilms.com/featured-filmmakers/aurora-guerrero/.

Li, Justin. "Inside Out 2012: Mosquita y Mari is an essay on young love that unquestionably makes the grade." *Popoptiq*, 2012, https://www.popoptiq.com/inside-out-2012-mosquita-y-mari-is-an-essay-on-young-love-that-unquestionably-makes-the-grade/.

"Meet the 2012 Sundance Filmmakers #42: Aurora Guerrero, 'Mosquita y Mari'". *IndieWire*, https://www.indiewire.com/2012/01/meet-the-2012-sundance-filmmakers-42-aurora-guerrero-mosquita-y-mari-49794/.

Mosquita y Mari Press Kit. Sundance Film Festival.

Pertusa, Inmaculada & Lourdes Torres, Eds. (2003). *Tortilleras. Hispanic and U.S. Lesbian Expression*, Philadelphia, Temple University Press.

Rich, Adriene (1994). "Notes toward a Politics of Location." *Blood, Bread and Poetry. Selected Prose 1979–1986*, New York. W.W. Norton & Company.

Saito, Steven. (2012). "'Mosquita y Mari': Pursuing Life, Liberty and Happiness With a Chicana Edge." *Takepart*, https://news.yahoo.com/news/mosquita-y-mari-pursuing-life-liberty-happiness-chicana-070000900.html.

Skogrand, Linda. & Hatch, Daniel. (2005). *Understanding Latino Families: Implications for Family Education*. Utah State University, Family Resources.

When Labels Don't Fit: Hispanics and Their Views of Identity, *Pew Research Center*, Hispanic Trends, 2012, https://www.pewresearch.org/hispanic/2012/04/04/when-labels-dont-fit-hispanics-and-their-views-of-identity/

CHAPTER 10

Pelo Malo (Mariana Rondón. 2013, Venezuela)

Abstract Mariana Rondón sets her successful film *Pelo Malo* in the heart of the city of Caracas, Venezuela. The country is suffering the health crisis of its then-authoritarian president Hugo Chávez, serving as a background to another crisis, one more individual and intimate. While "Chavismo" helped create a nationalism that affected gender activism, allowing more women to participate in the national guard and local police forces, it also profoundly ingrained authoritarian masculinity that pushed a new female workforce to the margins when the crisis began and work started to become scarce. This chapter analyzes how this socio-political context affects the lives of Martha and Junior, the family at the center of this film. The aspects analyzed focus on the construction of Junior's queer identity and how Martha reacts to it and on approaches that demonstrate Rondón's goal to offer a different reading of family, gender identification, and the social pressures that stifle any identity development.

Keywords Coming of age • Motherhood • LGBTQ • Family • Afro-Venezuelan • Venezuelan cinema

Production

Production	FiGa Films, Sudaca Films, World Cinema Fund, Global Film Initiative, CNAC, Ibermedia
Genre	Drama
Duration	93 minutes
Director	Mariana Rondón
Cinematography	Micaela Cajahuaringa
Producers	Marité Ugas, José Ibáñez, Gunter Hanfgarn, Carmen Rivas
Script	Mariana Rondón
Film Editing	Marité Ugas, Yovanny Leal
Sound	Cristian Berruezo, Francisco Pedemonte, John Figueroa, Lena Esquenazi
Music	Camilo Froideval

Cast

Junior	Samuel Lange Zambrano
Marta	Samantha Castillo
Carmen	Nelly Ramos
La Niña	María Emilia Sulbarán
El Jefe	Beto Benites

Synopsis

Junior is a ten-year-old boy that needs to take his school picture before the start of the academic year. With his best friend, The Girl (La Niña), he goes to a photographer's studio. His friend wants her picture to have a Miss Venezuela background. Junior wants to be portrayed as a singer with straight hair. The photographer tells him he will look better in a military backdrop, with a red beret. Junior is stubborn and says no. His desire to have straight hair and to achieve an image of himself that is not expected from an Afro-Venezuelan boy brings him misunderstanding from his mother, overprotection from his grandmother, and a confusing time for him. His main desire is that he wants to fit in and he believes straightening his hair is part of belonging. These details mark the beginning of a journey in which racial, gender, and class discourses clash and flow through the body of a boy in search of his identity.

Director's Take: Mariana Rondón (1966–)

Mariana Rondón is a director, scriptwriter, and plastic artist. Born in Barquisimeto, Venezuela, she studied animation in Paris, France, and from 1987 to 1990, was part of the first graduating class of the International Film and Television School in Cuba. In 1991 she co-founded Sudaca Films with Marité Ugás, a platform that has helped them create award-winning films such as *Postales de Leningrado* (*Postcards from Leningrad*, 2007) and *Pelo Malo* (*Bad Hair*, 2013) (iffr.com; sansebastianfestival.com). Rondón's filmography is an exploration of relationships, either familial or romantic, always subjected to crisis due to the invisible forces ingrained in social expectations and historical conventions, particularly in Venezuela. When discussing *Pelo Malo*, Rondón commented: "Llevo mucho tiempo asfixiada por esos pequeños gestos, por esas cosas que pasan en la vida diaria venezolana, cómo el contexto social se ha metido en las familias, los amigos, creando una pequeña violencia que puede parecer chiquita, pero que suma y suma [I have been suffocated for a long time by those small gestures, by those things that happen in daily Venezuelan life, how the social context has gotten into families, friends, creating a small violence that may seem small but that adds up and adds up]" (García, elpais.com). The "small gestures," the "small violence," are pieces of daily life and relationships to which Rondón pays attention in her scripts and films because these are consequences of a bigger reality that have filtered in everybody's homes and families in Venezuela: the politics and policies of Chavismo culture.

Hugo Chávez came to power in 1999 and with him a complete shift in Venezuelan politics. Defending the ideals of the Bolivarian Revolution, Chávez appropriated Cuban ideologies and applied them to his government. Populism, nationalization of private businesses, and constant propaganda became part of his revolutionary brand. He was well aware of the neoliberal forces, however, that controlled the global economy; thus, he also tried to create free trade and bilateral agreements that reinforced his control of oil companies and kept mostly cordial relationships with the United States and the European Union. His influence in national communications and messaging was evident in his weekly program *Aló, Presidente*, a public platform from which he was able to consolidate his policies and control the government's narrative. This control of the narrative is what Mariana Rondón places at the center of her films and her productions. By focusing on the small stories and violence, she is criticizing Venezuela's politics, but mostly Chávez's push for power that trickles down into Venezuelan's private lives and in all governmental institutions, including national cinema with Chávez's creation of the Villa del Cine in 2005.

Rondón's narratives in her films follow mostly young characters in search of a place to belong, either in a family or a community. Children are usually seen as the future of a country, but what happens when these children are not following the country's expectations? What happens when they are not following the historical narrative created for them? These are some of the questions that Rondón brings in her filmography and that she attempts to answer by close observation through the camera lens, long shots of the scenery, and a focus on intense glances from one character to another. Her pace in the narrative is slow in order for the spectators to pay attention, to carefully follow each action and each gesture, and to embed themselves in the small narrative, control it, and place it in conflict with the big narrative that surrounds it.

COMMENTARY AND CONTEXT

To understand the narrative and discursive perspective of *Pelo Malo*, it is necessary to understand how the production was placed in the bureaucracy and cinematographic policies during the Hugo Chávez administration. Before Chávez, Venezuela struggled to produce quality films. After a short-lived success in the 1980s, productions had a downturn due to the lack of interest from the country's audiences and preference for more stylized Hollywood films. In 1993, with the start of wide neoliberal policies around Latin America, a law was passed in order to subsidize and support local productions and creators. The 1993 law, however, did not guarantee an essential piece for the cinema industry: exhibition and distribution, which was addressed under Chávez when, in 2006, he announced in *Aló, Presidente* his interest in reforming the cinematography law by creating the Villa del Cine. As affirmed by Michelle Farrell, Chávez saw an opportunity by "recognizing the power of the movies as active cultural products with the ability to teach as well as protect the nation, connecting films with revolutionary discourse" (372). After the controversy of the popular film *Secuestro Express* [*Express Kidnapping*] (2005) where violence and despair represented a similar despaired Venezuela, and inspired by the cinematographic initiative from the Instituto Cubano de Arte e Industria

Cinematográficos (ICAIC) in Cuba, Chávez acknowledged the power of film narrative as a way to promote his own version of it in Venezuela. In his announcement, he declared: "Venezuelan film will be for the world, as Bolívar said: 'Weapons of thought'–artillery of our culture, artillery of our essence ... we are going to make quality movies!" (cited in Farrell 371). Quality films, thus, are equivalent to the Venezuelan essence, an essence the Chávez government could control.

The cinematographic platform created did not displace the efforts already established since 1993 but worked with them in order to provide—either by chance or intentionally—a wider space for Venezuelan directors, producers, and creators. Instead of a vertical platform as applied in the Cuban ICAIC, the Venezuelan platform was horizontal, each initiative taking care of one piece of the production puzzle a cinematographic industry entails. As Farrell explains,

> [T]he previously mentioned Villa del Cine (2006) is the national production company; Amazonia Films (2006) is the national distributor; the National Autonomous Cinematography Center (CNAC) (1993) is the financial arm of the industry; the Cinemateca Nacional (1966) is the national archive and exhibitor; and the National Disc Center (CENDIS) (2007) is the reproducer of discs and copies (for both films and music). (378)

Pelo Malo was created among all these new initiatives and reformulation of the cinematographic platform in Venezuela, especially with the support of the CNAC and in opposition to the Villa del Cine.

The Villa del Cine and the CNAC are the main institutions that support, both financially and creatively, the work of Venezuelan producers and directors. The mission of each, however, is different, and although it may overlap in resources, it does not do so in its objectives. The CNAC was created in 1993 and it was reformulated in 2005. It organizes and provides direct funding to both established and new directors. This funding comes from a combination of state support and private-sector investments. Directors and producers apply for this support with complete scripts and proposals that are evaluated by a private committee composed of members who have no relationship to the State. Films such as *Azul y no tan rosa* [*My Straight Son*] (2012) and *Pelo Malo* were produced under the CNAC's support.

Contrary to the approach from the CNAC, the Villa del Cine is highly dependent on state support and its mission is related to the government's ideologies. A committee recommends themes, mostly related to the Bolivarian Revolution, and creators would apply by submitting full proposals under such themes. This limitation of the Villa del Cine was highly criticized as it also limited creative freedom, but it was nevertheless a creative venue, especially for directors, producers, and actors who needed an organized medium and institution that would place Venezuelan productions at the center of film exhibition and distribution. Films like *Libertador* (2013) and *Miranda regresa* [*Miranda Returns*] (2007) focused on historical heroes, like Simón Bolívar and Francisco de Miranda, reframed under the perspective of the Bolivarian Revolution.

Many of the films related to the CNAC and the Villa del Cine are highly stylistic and have won awards and critical recognition around the world. The contention between these two platforms, although not reflected in the support given to its creators, was present in the media and the press, and the conflict some interviews triggered. *Pelo Malo* is an example of how these controversies transcend the cultural specter and became political fronts that defied Chavismo and its desire to control all narratives.

Between Narratives: The Small Gestures of Chavismo

Pelo Malo is an intimate portrayal of a family struggling to survive poverty. Junior, an Afro-Venezuelan boy, is the protagonist, and his obsession with straightening his curly hair creates intersections between discourses of race, gender, sexuality, and class. His mother, Marta, lost her job as a security guard and she is trying to get it back while confronting patriarchal attitudes that are limiting her options as a single mother of two children. While Junior is obsessing with his hair, Marta becomes preoccupied with her fear that Junior might be gay. Marta's fears do not take a turn into explicit violence, but into small, yet violent gestures that take a toll and challenge Junior's desires until they are completely repressed and displaced. The plot develops while Hugo Chávez is sick with cancer, referenced in the constant news clips presented on TV when the characters are watching it. To some extent, the film depicts dysfunctional family dynamics. The constant references to Chávez, either by bringing the news up or by the patriarchal images that remind the viewer that these family dynamics are not happening in a vacuum, Rondón is also confronting government ideologies and discourses.

After winning the Concha de Oro in the San Sebastian International Film Festival, in Spain, Rondón referenced the political climate that her film indirectly portrays through the mother and son relationship. To a question if her film was a representation of post-Chavismo politics under the new Venezuelan President that succeeded Chávez, Nicolás Maduro, Rondón replies: "No me gusta la polarización de mi país. Quiero que gente muy diferente encuentre ese lugar para charlar. En esta radicalización que me preocupa mucho hemos perdido los sitios de encuentro [I don't like the polarization of my country. I want people from different backgrounds to find a space to chat. During this radicalization, that worries me so much, we have lost our common meeting spaces]" (García, elpais.com). Lamenting the loss of common ground, Rondón is portraying her film as a cultural space in which she wants to have such dialogues, about race, homophobia, and social class. In another interview, when commenting about the inclusion of the news clips in her film, the director affirms:

> It was important to include those sequences, not just for context to fill in the setting, but because it was an important civic and political moment. People became fanatics, almost religiously so. That universe is where our story takes place. It's like a distinct form of violence, too. Violence in a social context ends up being reflected in the homes of friends and family. It always translates into the home. (Castillo, slantmagazine.com)

An example of such fanaticism is that people were shaving their heads in solidarity with Chávez who lost his hair due to cancer. Rondón's comments were not well received by many of her colleagues in Venezuela who criticized her for supposedly biting the hand that fed her, in reference to the funding she received by the cinematographic platform (Hernández, caracaschronicles.com), even if that funding was mostly from private investments through Sudaca Productions—Rondón's own production company—and the CNAC's non-related state initiatives. A blurring of the lines between creative initiatives from the cinematographic platform and politics was happening and *Pelo Malo* was caught in the crossfire. Nevertheless, the film created opportunities for conversations about race, gender, and class not achieved in other films and it presents a Venezuela that was falling to the small violent gestures triggered by political polarization and a lack of social empathy.

Queerness and Race: Junior's Struggle

A crucial scene for Junior happens at the beginning of the film. He and his best friend, The Girl (La Niña), go to the only photo studio affordable to them in their barrio. Precariousness is represented throughout the whole film, especially in the photo studio the children visit. Armed with a cellphone camera and a computer, the photographer creates illusions for the kids who need their photo for their school ID. While The Girl wants to dress up as Miss Venezuela, Junior wants to be a singer with straight hair and to have a waterfall as a background; instead, he confronts the photographer who puts him in a red beret and tells him he could be a soldier. Junior's resistance to this hypermasculine representation is important but also the fact that the sample picture presented to him is of a soldier who is a Black boy, with extremely short hair and who seems happy to be part of a military campaign. Instead, the boy that Junior wants to imitate is represented as white with longer, straight hair, and the background looks like a pleasant place. Race and status are discourses in conflict in Junior's imagination. His current status as a poor Afro-Venezuelan boy living in public housing in Caracas places him in danger—as he reminds The Girl by asking her to not stop anywhere while walking to the photo studio. Being a Black boy in Venezuela is also limiting, as he is immediately defined as a soldier rather than as a singer, which is his wish. Just like his friend, Junior is influenced by beauty standards and a subconscious understanding of what winning looks like: Europeanized, white, and with straight hair. His desire to be seen as part of the entertainment industry—a singer instead of a soldier—is a type of negotiation he has made with masculine expectations and his own desires.

While Marta, his mother, is looking for a job, Junior and his brother stay with their grandmother, Carmen. These two women do not get along; Carmen implies that Junior's baby brother is not from the same father. Marta needs her and prefers to not engage her, and when Carmen offers her money to keep Junior with her forever, Marta resists.

> Carmen: Yo te puedo ayudar con Junior. Dámelo y yo te lo crío. Pero me lo quedo para mí [I can help you with Junior. Give him to me, I'll raise him. But I'll keep him with me].
>
> Marta: (Impatient.) Carmen, yo te estoy pidiendo que te quedes con ellos un solo día. Nada más. Si te lo dejo, me lo van a matar en un par de años [Carmen, I am asking you to keep them for only one day. Not more

than that. If I leave him with you, they are going to kill him in a couple of years].
    Carmen: No, él es distinto. Él no tiene armas. Él sólo quiere ser bonito y arreglarse. Y eso a ti no te gusta [No, he is different. He does not have weapons. He just wants to be pretty and dress up. And that doesn't please you].
    Marta: Eso no es verdad [That is not true].
    Carmen: ¿Y entonces? ¿Qué fue lo que pasó en carnaval? [And then? What happened during the carnival?]
    Marta: (Concerned. Makes sure Junior is not close by.) Los carnavales son pa' eso Carmen [That's what carnivals are for, Carmen].
    Carmen: (Smirks, not convinced.) Piénsalo, Marta. Yo te doy plata y tú me das a Junior [Think about it, Marta. I'll give you money and you give me Junior].

Junior's desires have been at the forefront of both women's concerns since the time of the carnival. Although the spectator does not know what happened, the implication is that Junior made an attempt to come out during the carnival, at least from Carmen's perspective. Marta does not like this implication, she is always vigilant and questions Junior every time he performs out of what she thinks are masculine expectations. We learn later that apparently Junior's father was a victim of gun violence and was murdered. Junior is different, and Marta knows that he values being white and what he considers "pretty." Thus, "Junior lives under the racialized regime of aesthetics that values whiteness in Venezuela, which informs his valuation of his hair as ugly and in need of straightening. Yet, his mother reads this desire to straighten his hair through the lens of sexuality. Wanting to straighten his hair is one sign for his mother among many that Junior is gay" (Gillam 56). Just like guns, Marta knows that Junior's potential queerness may kill him, but more than protecting him, she imposes her patriarchal values, which Junior does not fully understand, since he does not understand his own desires beyond wanting to straighten his hair.

    This ambivalence in how Junior's sexuality is portrayed in the film is part of the small gestures that Rondón prefers to highlight in her films. Marta and Carmen are imposing their own discursive expectations of masculinity on Junior. Marta prefers him to assume a macho, protector role, while Carmen encourages his queer performance. Still, there is no clear conclusion, as Junior reacts to each imposition with resistance. As a mere ten-year-old, he is still searching for who he is: "The child is precisely who we [adults] are not and, in fact, never were. It is the act of adults looking back … 'we cannot know the contours of children, who they are to themselves,' and yet we must pretend that we do, acting in what we believe to be their best interest until the law considers them to be adults, legally responsible for their own existence" (St-Georges 296–297). When the institution of the family works as a national allegory, children have the responsibility of the future; they are trusted to continue or better the ideals already performed by their mother and their father (even if he is absent). This imposition creates expectations of these children that are limited to what adults project on them. What, then, happens when children do not follow these expectations?

Gender and Queerness: Marta's Struggle

Although most of the reviews and academic articles focus on Junior's struggle with race, class, and sexuality, less attention has been given to Marta's own challenges. In her actions and interactions with Junior, Marta does not perform the traditional roles of motherhood and she is villainized by her lack of empathy. Junior, however, looks at her with compassion and is willing to give up his wish to sing for her. This last action could be interpreted as Marta's triumph and the erasure of his desires. She understands how violence works—her husband was shot and murdered—and she knows that Junior will be bullied and hurt if he does not perform according to his gender. Marta has dealt with her own gender discrimination at her job and she has been violently placed, as a woman, in a vulnerable situation. As a widow and a single mother, throughout the film, she is pursuing the validation of her work as a security guard—a job traditionally performed by men—her only option is to perform according to her gender and sexuality.

Marta's characterization does not fulfill the expectations of motherhood or womanhood. She is not tender nor affectionate toward Junior, and she does not pay attention to her makeup, her clothing, or her physical posture. Often, she is portrayed as masculine, aggressive, and moody. The exception of this behavior happens with Junior's baby brother, who is still under Marta's full control. With Junior, she is vigilant, always wondering why her son acts the way he does. Her despair comes into focus when she visits Junior's pediatrician. She inquires if he might be gay and puts into words her concern by asking "Él va a sufrir, ¿verdad? [He is going to suffer, right?]." She asked if Junior's "condition" (as if it were a malady) may be because of her because she never caressed him. The doctor is confused and tells her that she needs to spend more time with her kids. Right after, she asks: "Y el pelo, ¿se lo corto? [and his hair, should I cut it?]." The doctor becomes impatient and tells her to take Junior out, to show him a father figure, "que el vea que puede existir una relación de amor entre un hombre y una mujer [for him to see that there can be a loving relationship between a man and a woman]." Marta receives all this advice and acts upon it.

Marta has not been able to secure her job through ethical means. She attempted to speak to her boss, but he never wanted to meet with her. Her last resort was to invite him over for dinner and to have sex with him. By shedding the last layer of her dignity, Marta is able to get her job back and, in her mind, follow the doctor's orders. When having sex with her boss in her living room, she leaves Junior's bedroom door open for him to observe this sexual encounter. She considers this a small gesture (though violent) that will make it clear to Junior that he needs to behave like a macho man and that she will not allow him to be gay. As Pierre Bourdieu argues, "[symbolic violence is] gentle violence, imperceptible and invisible even to its victims, exerted for the most part through the purely symbolic channels of communication and cognition ..., recognition, or even feeling ... the logic of domination exerted in the name of a symbolic principle known and recognized both by the dominant and by the dominated" (cited in Farrell 194). Marta does not need to physically abuse Junior to control him, but she constantly and violently reminds him that his behavior is unwanted. This symbolic violence entails not only what Marta thinks is a role model of a relationship for Junior but a way to repress his still unknown desires by putting her body in literal submission to patriarchal rule.

Although Marta cannot deal with Junior's behavior and latent queerness, she still resists Carmen's proposal to adopt him, but she uses this offer to entrap Junior. Marta feels like she has finally regained some power since she has managed to get her job back. One morning, after a long night shift, she prepares Junior his favorite meal and makes it obvious that she has his belongings packed and ready. Junior is simultaneously happy and worried. He asks about the bag and Marta tells him she has decided to allow him to go live with Carmen. He refuses and promises to never sing again. Marta does not listen. He then asks about the possibility of cutting his hair. She was ready for him to make this offer knowing that he would want to stay so she immediately took out an electric hair clipper. There is a pause in their dialogue until Junior tells her "No te quiero [I don't love you]" and for Marta to respond "Yo tampoco [neither do I]." The dining area where this scene takes place parallels the scene in the doctor's office. Both rooms are lit with natural lighting coming in through the windows, highlighting the cool colors. The emptiness of the dining room also creates a sterile environment like the doctor's examination room. Although the doctor assured her that her son did not have a disease, she has disregarded this information. The shaving of Junior's hair is like a "medical procedure"; she "treats" his behavior by removing the supposed root of the problem, Junior's hair. Marta is the authority figure in the room, dressed in her uniform. She does not advise Junior, as the doctor did to her, but instead forces him to shave his "pelo malo." His "bad hair" is not only a symbol of his African heritage and alleged lack of European beauty, but it is also a bad influence that has condemned him, in Marta's eyes, to be a victim of violence and homophobia given his potential queerness. By emotionally bribing Junior, Marta was, in her mind, saving him from violence. He never had an opportunity to choose what he wanted to be. Influenced by a society that marginalized and brutalized her as well, Marta, as his mother, made sure Junior would remain under the expectations and the narrative selected for him.

Bibliography

"Mariana Rondón." *IFFR*, https://iffr.com/en/persons/mariana-rond%C3%B3n.
"Mariana Rondón." *San Sebastián International Film Festival*, 62nd edition, 19–27 September 2014, https://www.sansebastianfestival.com/2014/premios_y_jurados/1/4370/in.
Bad Hair [Pelo Malo]. IMDB, https://www.imdb.com/title/tt3074610/fullcredits/?ref_=tt_cl_sm
Castillo, Mónica. "Interview: Mariana Rondón Talks *Bad Hair*." *Slant*, 19 Nov. 2014, https://www.slantmagazine.com/film/interview-mariana-rondon/.
Farrell, Michelle Leigh. "A Close-Up on National Venezuelan Film Support During the Chávez Years: Between Revolution and Continuity." *The Latin Americanist*, Vol. 60, No. 3, 2016, pp. 371–390. *Wiley Online Library*, DOI: https://doi.org/10.1111/tla.12084.
Farrell, Michelle Leigh. "Pelo malo: Representing Symbolic Violence in the Intricacies of Venezuela Contemporary Film Landscape." *Cincinatti Romance Review*, Vol. 42, spring 2017, pp. 190–210. *Digital Commons at Fairfield*, https://digitalcommons.fairfield.edu/modernlanguagesandliterature-facultypubs/31?utm_source=digitalcommons.fairfield.edu%2Fmodernlanguagesandliterature-facultypubs%2F31&utm_medium=PDF&utm_campaign=PDFCoverPages.

García, Rocío, and Gregorio Belinchón. "Chávez nos sentenció a la guerra." *El País*, 28 Sept. 2013, https://elpais.com/cultura/2013/09/28/actualidad/1380390514_383994.html.

Gillam, Reighan. "All Tangled Up: Intersecting Stigmas of Race, Gender, and Sexuality in Mariana Rondón's Bad Hair." *Black Camera*, Vol. 9, No. 1, fall 2017, pp. 47–61. *JSTOR*, https://www.jstor.org/stable/10.2979/blackcamera.9.1.03.

Hernández A., Gustavo. "The curious case of Mariana Rondón." *Caracas Chronicles*, 9 Oct. 2013, https://www.caracaschronicles.com/2013/10/09/the-curious-case-of-mariana-rondon/.

CHAPTER 11

Bruising for Besos (Adelina Anthony, 2016, USA)

Abstract In her debut and independently produced film *Bruising for Besos*, Xicana queer writer, actor, director, and producer Adelina Anthony plays the role of the protagonist, Yoli Villamontes, who confronts present and past domestic violence as she attempts to "build familia from scratch" with other queer and trans people of color in Los Angeles, California. Yoli, a Xicana jota (queer) originally from Texas, has left her biological family behind to pursue her art in California. Anthony names her after "Yolotl" (the word for "heart" in Nahuatl) because Yoli travels through life with a giving and open heart that betrays her as she falls into a physically abusive relationship with her Puerto Rican lover Daña (a name which translates as someone who hurts others). This relationship replicates the violent episodes from Yoli's parents that traumatized her as a small child. This chapter focuses on a survivor of Latinx queer domestic and intimate partner violence, on Xicana queer Indigenous identity, and art as healing. Anthony takes advantage of her decades of experience in theater and performance as she offers her masterful directorial debut in what promises to be the first of a series of films by AdeRisa Productions, a company she co-founded with her partner, Marisa Becerra.

Keywords Lesbianism • Lesbian • Family • Domestic violence • Chicana • Chicanx

Production

Production	Adelina Anthony, Marisa Becerra, AdeRisa Productions, LLC
Genre	Drama
Duration	86 minutes
Director	Adelina Anthony
Cinematography	Catalina Ausin
Producers	Adelina Anthony and Marisa Becerra, executive producers/producers; José M. Aguilar-Hernández, Julián Hernández, Lorenzo Herrera y Lozano, Karla Legaspy, Irene Mata, Cristina Serna, and Aimee Carrillo Rowe, co-producers; Catalina Ausin, Miguel Angel Caballero, Jo Ann Castillo, Grace Chang, Denise Contreras, D'Lo, Alyssa Flores, Genevieve Flores, Aurora Garcia, Gaye Theresa Johnson, Stacy Macias, Marissa Medina, Brigitt Montes, Augie Robles, Maria Salazar, Audrey Silvestre, Judy Sisneros, and Cynthia Velásquez, associate producers
Script	Adelina Anthony
Film Editing	Augie Robles
Sound	Adolfo Maure Giacchetti, Juan Manuel Mesa, Nicolás Osorio, Bethany Tucker, Sebastián Vivas
Music	Alex Valenzy

Cast

Yoli	Adelina Anthony
Daña	Carolyn Zeller
Rani	D'Lo
Carmela (and Little Sister)	Natalie Camunas
Ixchel	Marlene Beltran Cuauhtin
Imani (and Little sister)	Lawrencia Dandridge
Nerea (and abuela)	Brenda Banda

Synopsis

Yoli, a young Xicana butch lesbian artist originally from Texas, is dreaming of a new life in the City of Los Angeles, California. While living with her best friend, Rani, she is working on an artistic project that may bring her new opportunities. She has also created a new chosen queer family, in the city, composed of friends and colleagues. On her birthday, Yoli meets and falls in love with Daña, a Puerto Rican Catholic nurse who struggles with her queer identity. Throughout this relationship, Yoli's life takes a turn in regard to her past while dealing with Daña's abusive relationship in the present, breaking away from her chosen family, struggling with her biological family, and threatening her future due to domestic violence.

Director's Take: Adelina Anthony (1973–)

Originally from the southside of San Antonio, Texas, Adelina Anthony's art, whether on the theater stage or in film, strives to represent the lives, challenges, and triumphs of queer and trans people of color (QTPOC) primarily in the U.S. southwest, with special emphasis on southern California and central/south Texas. On her website, she/they states, "I live & work on occupied Tongva lands. I am a two spirit, genderqueer Xicana/x lesbian feminist artist working on behalf of my peoples: past, present, and future. I/we create projects intended for intergenerational healing, resistance, dialogue, and pleasure." Anthony's artistic origins begin as a writer/playwright, director, and actor. She received her B.A. in Drama from the University of Dallas and her Master of Arts, also in Drama, from Stanford University under the tutelage of Chicana lesbian author/playwright Cherríe Moraga. Initially, Anthony had a prolific career in theater and performance and received numerous awards as an actor, director, and writer. Earlier in her/their theater career, she/they toured several performance art pieces throughout the United States, such as *Mastering Sex and Tortillas* (a hilarious approach to Chicana queerness), *Tragic Bitches* (a poetic performance about the pain and struggles of Xicana queer love and intrafamily violence, in collaboration with queer Xicanx poets Dino Foxx and Lorenzo Herrera y Lozano), and *La Hocicona Series*, a comedic triptych that includes *La Angry Xicana, La Sad Girl*, and *La Chismosa*. In 2003, while working with Moraga, Anthony developed *Bruising for Besos* (*B4B*) originally as a solo play, as a story of a Xicana femme-macha's survival and loss of self and her tumultuous relationship with her mother who is dying. *Bruising for Besos* was later transformed and re-written for its film version.

In 2012, Anthony participated in the Fusion Lab by Outfest, a Los Angeles-based organization that supports queer arts, media, and entertainment. That same year she/they wrote, directed, and co-produced her/their first short film about intimacy and friendship between two teenage girls titled *Forgiving Heart*. It premiered the following year at the Outfest Fusion Queer People of Color Film Festival Gala. In 2013, during her/their fellowship at Film Independent's Project Involve, while working with story editor Ruth Atkinson, Anthony wrote her/their second short film *You're Dead to Me* (about a grieving Chicana mother who receives a visit by Death on Day of the Dead and has to make some challenging choices). It won the Imagen Award in 2014. In 2013, her/their first feature-length film was *Bruising for Besos*, which she/they developed under the Sony Diversity Fellowship and a year later, the participation in the Sundance Screenwriters Intensive program brought together a team that included Joan Tewkesbury and Guinevere Turner to work with Anthony. The film version of *Bruising for Besos* intentionally highlights the butch character of Yoli in order to confront the scarcity of masculine-of-center characters in general and of butch Chicana/Chicanx characters in particular in film and television. Additionally, Rani as a trans male character is also purposely included in the film version to challenge transphobia in Chicanx/Latinx and other communities of color as well as in general.

In 2012, Anthony and her partner Marisa Becerra created AdeRisa Productions, LLC to support films by and for LGBTQ+ folks, people of color, and allies. Since then, AdeRisa Productions, Marisa Becerra, and Adelina Anthony have supported collectively, individually, and in various roles, the production of over a dozen films of various lengths. Their latest production is developing *La Seranata* [*The Serenade*], an award-winning short film produced in 2019 in collaboration with RebozoBoy Productions into a feature-length film. *La Serenata* is about a young Chicano boy who wants to serenade another boy and the way in which his traditional family reacts to his request and allow their love for their child to triumph. Adelina Anthony's and AdeRisa's cinematic representations by queer and trans people of color consistently have garnered various awards, which demonstrate the need for such stories to continue to be represented.

Commentary and Context

Before becoming a film, *Bruising for Besos* was a one-woman show created for the stage and performed by Adelina Anthony. It "premiered in 2009 at the Los Angeles Gay and Lesbian Center earning Anthony a nomination for Best Solo Performance from *LA Weekly*" (Sanchez n.p.). The show featured Anthony as Yoli, who reminisces about her life via flashbacks while stuck on the highway and waiting for help with her car, which broke down in the southwest U.S. desert while she is on her way back to Texas to visit her dying mother one last time. According to Anthony, "[i]t's a real portrait of a life, of surviving poverty and surviving domestic violence" (Abney). This same approach of a portrait of a life is represented in the film. The flashbacks, however, do not happen as real-life memories but through an art project with puppets on which Yoli is working. The film opens with a family scene of a birthday party where everyone is represented by puppets. Young Yoli is celebrating with her mom, dad, brother, and baby sister. It looks like an ideal celebration. Instead of the Hot Wheels cars she wanted, however, Yoli receives one more doll as a gift. Her dad attempts to comfort her by giving her five dollars, and she wonders if she can buy a toy car with that money. Then we hear the sound of an alarm and we observe the real Yoli waking up, turning it off, picking up Yoli the puppet, and smiling. The previous scene was a dream, but it was a pleasant one. Then, the focus is on a painting on the wall representing two women, lying side by side and one seems to be masturbating. In this brief introduction, the main theme of a "portrait of a life" in the film is established, visually providing what the play recreated in flashbacks: the centrality of family, particularly Yoli's relationship with her dad, her queerness, and the gender expectations imposed on her.

From the play in 2009 to the film in 2016, the script went through multiple iterations and revisions, thanks to a Sundance Intensive Writers Workshop in 2014. In a publication of the original play in *Chicana/Latina Studies*, Anthony explains,

> I am writing these pieces with a personal and communal intention. They are first and foremost the offerings I promised my mother–that I would take the experience of what she and my family have survived (and also what we haven't survived) in order to make peace with the legacies of violence I inherited. But these are not necessarily auto-dramas; they are fiction; they are art; they are spirit work. These plays take up the knowledge of surviving domestic violence, and through the transgressive process of honest art-making, I allow the story to shape itself. (Anthony 2010, 62)

This primary intention is also sensed in the film as the puppet scenes reflect Yoli's familial life and inner conflicts without bringing them to the fore of her reality. Family history and her own present life intersect and clash, but it is the spectator who is able to make these connections. Thus, in the "process of honest art-making," the film provides the audience with clues to understand Yoli, but this is not the only way in which she can be understood. Her choices and how the story "shapes itself" develop a different side of her that gives her complexity and depth, which are often ignored in other queer portrayals, especially in Latinx cinematic representations.

In the film, Anthony explores two sides of Yoli: one that is dealing with being a queer, butch subject, and another that remains haunted by the trauma of domestic violence during her childhood. In a conversation with her roommate, Rani, Yoli defends her trail of failed relationships such as the one she had with Imani. Yoli states: "You know, when we come out it's like we are teenagers all over again, except we need to deal with homo or transphobia, right? As we grow through our fucking queer skin. So, who gets it right Rani?" While acknowledging her queer identity is still in development, Yoli excuses her bad choices in her past relationships that, in the words of Rani, have hurt her. She is, after all, still affected and influenced by her family's violent past. This supposed immaturity, especially during a moment of weakness and desperation, will lead Yoli to attempt to kiss Carmela, Rani's girlfriend, damaging the trust and friendship between everyone involved.

The Past in the Present in Reflection of the Future Through Puppets

Adelina Anthony creates an effective parallel narrative in *Bruising for Besos* by including the old theatrical technique of the play within a play (or a film, in this case). There are two story lines and as they both develop they begin to intersect in the actions and decisions taken by Yoli. One story is about the struggles she faces in her life in L.A., dealing with an unfulfilling and badly paying job, her unsuccessful romantic relationships, and her estrangement from her biological family. The other is about young Yoli and her family, seen through the puppets that the real Yoli is recreating for an art project. Opening the film with a scene from this artistic approach is a signal to the audience that they need to pay attention to the dynamics portrayed in this peculiar way because it creates a certain emotional distance. Yoli as a child grows up in a home that turns violent and where various types of betrayals are presented. By representing her story through the puppets, Anthony does not need to provide the violent reenactment by flesh and blood actors regarding her childhood memories. According to Ronald D. Burgess in his analysis of the Mexican companies La Trouppe and Marionetas de la Esquina, the use of puppets allows for "dreams, a disregard for linear time, and from a magical world where imagination, daydreams, fantasies, and everyday objects come to life. The necessary suspension of disbelief is easier for an audience that has already agreed to accept puppets as animated and even living beings" (100). On that same note, Yoli's past by way of puppets provides a window to these memories without the pitfalls of violent melodrama that may distract from her reality in Los Angeles.

The different puppetry scenes are interjected with the main storyline as a way to understand Yoli's reaction to a situation, an action, or a reaction from her colleagues, friends, and, especially, her lover Daña. An illustrative scene that depicts this interjection is the one that happens right after Rani warns Yoli about her current partner. Yoli has attempted and failed to communicate with her. She decides to drive by Daña's house and to check on her. When parking and getting her jacket, she finds Yoli the puppet and asks her "Hey, how did you get in here?" She immediately notices a car parked and a man, whom she does not recognize, comes out of Daña's house, making Yoli suspicious. She decides to go investigate and have a conversation with her lover. The camera stays on her when getting out of the car and slowly moves back to Yoli the puppet, lying on the dashboard. Once inside the home, Yoli decides to confront Daña, who by then is taking a bath. She demands an explanation regarding the man she saw and her lover states that he is a nurse that was helping her dad, who had suddenly become sick. Yoli sarcastically points out how convenient of a situation it is and raises her voice. Daña starts yelling at her and slaps her but immediately, becomes apologetic, blaming her for supposedly driving her crazy. Yoli leaves and goes to a bar. The story switches to a puppet scene at a bus station. We see young Yoli's mom crying, her face is bruised. Yoli attempts to make her laugh, but her mom is not having it. They are on their way to move to Houston from San Antonio. Yoli had said she would stay with her Abuela but became afraid and left with her mom. While leaving the bus station, a young African-American kid asks her grandmother: "Granny, who hit that lady in the face?" to which her grandmother answers, "Someone who don't know how to love right, baby," and the scene ends.

Having these two scenes connected in the editorial montage provides Anthony with a space for reflection and for bringing the audience to Yoli's state of mind. What happened with Daña triggered a memory that we see in the puppets, a memory representing a cycle of violence from which Yoli has been trying to run away. Although Anthony is recreating these two aspects of Yoli's life, they do not interconnect but run parallel. To some extent, Anthony is providing the audience with more knowledge than what the main character offers. The audience, then, begins to care for Yoli. This point is crucial in the development of a queer play/film. As Venkatesh proposes, some films encourage a "circulation of empathy" concerning queer characters (61). In that sense, it is a film that interacts with the spectators, breaking the "safe distance" (62) between the film and the spectator. At the same time, Anthony is able to create a story that appeals to a universal audience. Her story of struggle and survival is one that goes beyond the specificities of Anthony's background as Xicana/x and queer/two spirit. As she/they states in an interview with *Remezcla*:

> We're still working at a political spectrum where the white writer, the one that has been historically given the privilege of writing and making stories, they're set up to be like "Oh everything they do is imaginative" because they're the heteronormative, they're the universal. And so when we write: "Oh it must come from their very specific experience" which quite often it does but we're also highly invested in the creative act. (Valdés)

Anthony's creative act delves into the psychological appreciation for Yoli by observing, with the tenderness a puppetry show brings, how Yoli grew up and how her life was turned upside down.

Pronouncing Queer Desire

From the beginning, it is clear that the narrative and visual aspects of this film contradict the heteronormative matrix. In *Bruising for Besos* the cinematic language serves to dislocate the traditional point of view through innovative angles and use of the camera. The first two minutes of the film focus on a drawing that depicts two naked women sexually enjoying each other. Right after, we see Yoli and her roommate going "somewhere," which happens to be Yoli's surprise birthday party hosted by their friend Ixchel. A diverse group of friends welcomes them, indicating that they are all part of the same "chosen family" for the *jotería* (queer friends and lovers). They are young Chicanx and Latinxs queers walking together in life, sharing the joy but also the trauma of growing up in a culture in which the traditional family is heteronormative per excellence. Often, being a Chicanx or Latinx queer is equivalent to being "exiled" from one's biological family. In this sequence, we can see Yoli enjoying herself with her queer family—and by queer we want to use a broad definition that includes all the manifestations of sexuality that disrupts and challenges the heteronormative matrix. Furthermore, the spectators are witnesses to the "pronouncement" of the lesbian/queer desire that, in most Latin American and Latinx films, has been erased. As Inmaculada Pertusa and Lourdes Torres indicate, there is a long tradition of "impronunciability" of lesbian and queer women's desires in the sociocultural discourse in Latin America and in the U.S. Latinx communities, as well as in Spain (Fig. 11.1).

Besides highlighting the concept of "chosen family," the initial sequence also centers queer desire. Yoli meets a mysterious woman, Daña, at her birthday party. She becomes the love interest of Yoli at the party and thereafter. At some point, we see Yoli looking at Daña for the first time, and the audience can guess the queer desire in both of them because of the way they look at each other. At the party, Daña appears to be by herself. The camera provides the spectators a long shot in which we see the party and when one of Yoli's friends begins to sing a romantic song. Right after, we see Daña walking toward a hidden garden, followed by Yoli. The camera adopts Yoli's point of view and we see that the target is her object of

Fig. 11.1 Daña and Yoli meet

desire: Daña. As she approaches her, the camera continues to represent Yoli's gaze by zooming in until they are close and then sitting in front of each other.

The spectators can feel the attraction between these two women, but the camera does not focus only on the bodies. As Laura Mulvey proposes, the majority of films and TV adopt what she calls the "male gaze," the point of view of the heterosexual male objectifying women and their bodies. In this case, we can hear a playful-serious dialogue where they introduce themselves and pronounce their desire for each other. Both are dressed in red, the color of desire, and the lights are low. Suddenly, the camera zooms in on Daña's face and we see her eyes and her smile. Carolyn Zeller, who plays the role of Daña, has an expressive face, big eyes, and we can hear Yoli complimenting her, "Damn, you have pretty eyes"; therefore, the lesbian/queer desire is beautifully expressed with the dialogue and cinematic language. In other words, queer desire is pronounced, finally, in a sociocultural discourse. At this point, they are in a "comfort zone" where they are able to express their desire: they are in a hidden garden, with their queer, chosen family. As Rita Urquijo-Ruiz indicates, there is a "queer zone of comfort [that is] created and inhabited by a Chicana/o and Latina/o queer subject after negotiating his/her identity conflicts" (138). If both characters will have to confront their historic traumas as queer Latinas, Adelina Anthony is creating this space of comfort throughout the film. Anthony dedicates this work to "Our ancestors, present day communities and generations to come." In this way she creates a space of comfort and, in this sense, she is a Xicanx *artívist* (artist and activist) through her films. As Urquijo-Ruiz argues, "[In] this queer zone of comfort, the subject must create familial and familiar unbreakable bonds with other members of his/her community who support social change for the betterment of the group" (138). Anthony, her film crew, and supporters believe in the power of community building and chosen families that make this queer work possible. AdeRisa Productions consistently calls upon their communities to collectively raise the necessary funds to not only produce high-caliber films but to pay their workers, artists, and actors honorable wages.

Daña, the Red Woman: Who Cannot be Controlled and Loses Control

Red is Daña's color, especially because she is a strong, provocative character. Her name, however, is already a warning in Spanish—"Daña" derives from the verb "dañar," which means "to hurt," but by wearing different shades of red, her whole body is both a warning and an enticement. In a symbolic act of engagement with the audience, Anthony is, again, providing more information to them than what Yoli knows. This act of metanarrative affects not only how the audience perceives Daña but what to expect from her and the frustration to watch Yoli succumb to violence time and again. As witnesses to a relationship that soon becomes abusive, the audience cannot do much for her, but to see how Yoli emerges, on her own, to her freedom. And that is Anthony's objective: to make us care but to also distance us by reminding the audience of the artificiality of the story. By applying Bertold Brecht's alienation effect, which "involves the use of techniques designed to distance the audience from emotional involvement in the play through jolting reminders of the artificiality of the theatrical performance" (Britannica Academic), in her film, Anthony is creating a third space for the audience to ask questions, to inquire, to be present but with some distance.

Daña is the embodiment of the artificial, as her presence is a complete performance, always ambivalent in how to relate to Yoli: is she her girlfriend or her friend? Defined by her Catholic beliefs, Daña punishes herself every time she gets too close to Yoli by snapping, creating drama, being jealous, and resorting to physical violence without thinking. She becomes Yoli's abuser. Without wanting to acknowledge it, the audience recognizes that this relationship parallels that of Yoli's parents. The puppets bring that part of the story to the forefront, but not to Yoli's mind or conscience. The puppets' performance is only for the benefit of the audience and Daña's persistence and apologetic persona is a performance for Yoli. The audience can perceive this behavior, but Yoli cannot allow herself to acknowledge such similarities.

Their relationship implodes and spins out of control when Yoli leaves, after one more episode in which Daña allows her Catholic guilt to impede her happiness and regrets being sexually involved with her female partner. After fighting, on one occasion, Yoli decides to have sex with Suzi, a coworker, who had been flirting with her. When she goes back to Daña's house to pick up her things, Daña acts as a "damsel in distress" and once again, Yoli falls for this performance. Still, Daña sees Yoli's phone with a missed call from Suzi and violently demands to find out details about this woman. She grabs Yoli by the hair and this action exposes a hickey. Daña is immediately enraged and loses control, screaming and slamming Yoli, who decides to leave with her things after Daña punches her, leaving her in a state of shock and attempting to recover. Daña cries and asks her not to go, but when Yoli refuses her apologies, she screams: "Fine! You wanna leave? Primero pégame [hit me]. Pégame like your papá used to hit your mamá." After the initial shock, Yoli is now the one who becomes violent but never hits Daña. She demands that her girlfriend explain the reason for her cruel mind games by mentioning her parents' violent relationship at that precise moment in the fight; unable to control her anger, Yoli punches the wall, which results in both of them crying in pain. This particular scene is a watershed moment in the plot and in Yoli's life. There is also a different cinematographic style that corresponds to the action that we spectators are watching: the camera seems to be unstable, extremely close to the subjects in dramatic and harmful movements.

In the following scene, Yoli is heartbroken because her life is upside down and her failed and violent relationship with Daña forcibly pushes her to confront her childhood trauma. She decides to give up her art by burning the puppets she had created with so much excitement. Hopeless, she gets drunk and runs away in her car, suffering an accident, which, together with her violent, failed relationship, pushes her to have a more honest relationship with herself. In this sense, Adelina Anthony creates an intricate narrative that enables the main character to have an epiphany in relation to her past, her affective relationships, and the circle of violence in which she has lived for most of her life. It is noteworthy that Anthony speaks about the hidden reality of many queer relationships that suffer from intrafamily and partner violence. According to the National Coalition Against Domestic Violence (2022), around 43.8% of lesbian women and 61.1% of bisexual women have experienced some degree of violence (stalking, rape, physical, and psychological) by an intimate partner. Domestic violence in the transgender community is more considerable. It is necessary to speak about the many traumas that affect the LGBTQ+ community: violence at home but also, and it is well-known, violence and discrimination in the public sphere. Speaking out about traumas enables the spectators to reflect on the sociocultural discourse that perpetuates dynamics of oppression between and against queer people of color. The last scene focuses on Rani and Yoli renewing their trust and friendship. As

Yoli is about to board her train, she gives a soft kiss to the only puppet she had kept, that of little Yoli, signifying the hope that she, forcibly, will begin the painful journey of healing her inner child from the decades of violence and trauma.

Bibliography

Abney, Andrea. "Bruising for Besos: Adelina Anthony's play." *SFGate*, https://www.sfgate.com/thingstodo/article/Bruising-for-Besos-Adelina-Anthony-s-play-3182517.php. Accessed 15 September 2022.

Anthony, Adelina. "Introduction: Bruising for Besos." *Chicana/Latina Studies*, Vol. 9, No. 2, Spring 2010, pp. 62–95.

Burgess, Ronald D. "Mexico City's (Almost) Invisible Family Theatre: Puppets at Work." *Latin American Theatre Review*, Vol. 38, No. 2, pp. 97–106.

Britannica, The Editors of Encyclopaedia. "Alienation effect." Encyclopedia Britannica, 7 Feb. 2020, https://www.britannica.com/art/alienation-effect. Accessed 22 October 2023.

Pertusa, Inmaculada & Lourdes Torres, Eds. (2003). *Tortilleras. Hispanic and U.S. Lesbian Expression*, Philadelphia, Temple University Press.

Sanchez, Sam. "Two Lesbian Films on Tap at CineFestival." *OutInSA*, February 2, 2017, https://outinsa.com/two-lesbian-films-tap-cine-festival/. Accessed 15 September 2022.

Urquijo-Ruiz, Rita E. (2014). "Coming home: The Latina/o queer zone of comfort." *Aztlán: A Journal of Chicano Studies,* Vol. 39, No. 1, pp. 247–252.

Valdés, Pili. "Queer Director Adelina Anthony Destroys the Myth that POC Filmmakers Can't Tell Universal Stories." *Remezcla*, August 9, 2016, https://remezcla.com/features/film/adelina-anthony-interview-bruising-for-besos/. Accessed 15 September 2022.

Venketash, V. *New Maricón Cinema,* University of Texas Press, 2016.

Index

A
Activism, xxi, 75
AdeRisa, 130, 136
Afro-Venezuelan, 114, 118–121
Agency, v, vi, xiii, xvi, 11, 43–47, 93
Anthony, Adelina, 136–138
Argentinian cinema, 31
Artivist, 136

B
Body, v, xvi, 5, 7, 10–13, 24, 25, 34, 35, 38, 44–46, 49, 57, 69–71, 80, 109, 110, 114, 123, 136, 137
Bratt, Peter, 66–67
Brincando el Charco, xvi, 17–21
Bruising for Besos, xxi, 134

C
Caribbean, vi, 17
Chavismo, xxi, 115–116, 118
Chicana(s), xx, 102–104, 106–107, 109, 111, 129, 130, 136
Chicano, 69, 103, 130

Chicanx, 67, 68, 130, 134
Cinema law, 55, 87
Class, 5, 19, 22, 34, 104, 110, 118, 119, 122
Colonial, 50
Colonialism, 21
Colonialist, 18
Coming of age, 104
Coming out, xx, 25, 133
Community, xiii–xvii, xx, xxii, 17, 20, 43, 44, 67, 68, 75–77, 80–82, 91, 103–110, 116, 136, 138

D
Danzón, xvi, 5
Depatriarchalize/depatriarchalizing, xiv, xv
Desire(s), xvii, 4, 11–14, 25, 36, 37, 50, 59, 93, 102, 105, 107, 109, 110, 114, 118, 120–123, 134–136
Diaspora, 16–18, 20, 21, 23, 24, 75
Diversity, 23, 54, 67, 75, 80
Domestic violence, 129–132, 138
Dominican cinema, 87, 88

E

Ecuador, xiv, xviii, 52–61
Empower/empowering, xiii, 44, 50, 93, 104
Empowerment, 30, 50, 77–79, 103
Enjoy, 13, 60, 78, 79
Enjoyment, 12, 13, 57
Entre Nos, xix, 75–77, 82

F

Feminine, 9, 94
Feminist, 7, 50, 67, 88, 90, 93, 96, 129
Friendship, xx, 31, 39, 60, 102, 105, 106, 129, 132, 138

G

Gender performance, xviii
Gender roles, xiv, xx, 82, 90, 91, 93, 96
Golden Age of Mexican Cinema, 6–8
Guerrero, Aurora, 105, 106

H

Hermida, Tania, xviii, 53–54, 58
Heteronormative, vi, xiii, xv, xx, 6, 10, 25, 90, 134, 135
Heteropatriarchal system, 46, 47, 49, 50
Hollywood, 53
Homophobia, xiv, 16, 66, 71, 105, 124
Huntington Park, 104
Hybrid identities, 19–20

I

Ibermedia, 55
Immigration, 77, 82

Indigenous, xiv, xvii, xxi, 6, 9, 43–45, 55, 57, 66, 68, 71
Instituto Cubano de Arte e Industria Cinematográficos (ICAIC), 116–117
Intersectionality, xviii

L

La Hija Natural, xix, 86–91
La Mission, xviii–xix, 67
La Morte, Gloria, xix, 75–76, 81–82
Latina(s), xx, 77, 82, 106, 131, 136
Latino, 22, 67–71
Latino cinema, 71
Lerman, Diego, 30–32, 34
Lesbian, xvi, xvii, 21, 24–25, 37–39, 105–106, 128–131, 135, 136, 138
Lesbianism, 24, 37, 105
LGBTQ communities, 7, 9, 69–70, 138
Llosa, Claudia, 42–43

M

Madeinusa, xvii–xviii, 42
Magical realism, 93
Masculinity, xviii, xix, xxi, 10, 67–70, 94, 121
Melodrama/melodramatic, xvi, 92, 133
Mendoza, Paola, xix, 74–77, 81–82
Mexican cinema, 5–7
Minority, 21, 22, 25
Mosquita y Mari, xx, 102
Motherhood, 5, 75, 122
Mulvey, Laura, 12, 136

N

National cinema, 18, 55, 88, 116
National identity, xvi, 19, 21–22, 24, 25, 90

Negrón Muntaner, Frances, 16–18, 24, 25
Nostalgic, xvi, xviii, 6–8
Novaro, Beatriz, 7
Novaro, María, v, 4–6

P
Paredes, Julieta, xiv, xx
Patriarchy, xiv, xix, 92, 94
Pelo Malo, xx–xxi, 114
Performance, xvi, xxi, 6–9, 17–19, 23, 37, 70, 71, 121, 129, 130, 137, 138
Peruvian cinema, 43, 45
Politics of identity, 108
Postcolonial, 20, 50
Postmodern cinema, 33–34
Power, xiv, xvii, 10–12, 47, 48, 50, 102, 115–117, 123, 136
Puerto Rican cinema, 17, 18

Q
Queer, vi, xiii, xv, xxi, xxii, 17, 37, 69–70, 102–105, 120–124
Queer desire, 134–136
Queer gaze, xx, 17–20
Queerness, xiii, xvi, 18, 107, 120–124, 129, 131
Queer perspective, 17
Queer studies, 17, 70, 110
Qué Tan Lejos, xviii, 53–56, 58, 60

R
Race, xiv, 5, 19, 22, 67, 118–122
Religious, xvii, 42, 43, 48, 49

Road movie, xviii, 31–34, 36, 38, 55, 61
Rondón, Mariana, xx, xxi, 114–116, 119

S
Self-discovery, xx, 30, 32, 36, 108–111
Sexual freedom, xvii
Sexuality, vi, xiii, xvii–xviii, xx, 7, 8, 12–14, 16, 19–22, 24, 25, 37, 67, 69, 102, 104–106, 118, 121
Social conventions, xiv, 96

T
Tan de Repente, xvii, 32, 33, 36
Telenovelas, 90–93
Tonos, Leticia, 87–91, 93
Touristic, 54, 57–60
Toxic masculinity, 68
Traveling, xviii, 4, 11, 44, 52, 54–56, 58–60

V
Venezuelan cinema, 117
Virginity, 44–48

W
Womanhood, vi, xix, 7, 10, 11, 13, 122
Working-class, xvii, 7, 8, 67, 104

SPRINGER NATURE

GPSR Compliance

The European Union's (EU) General Product Safety Regulation (GPSR) is a set of rules that requires consumer products to be safe and our obligations to ensure this.

If you have any concerns about our products, you can contact us on ProductSafety@springernature.com

In case Publisher is established outside the EU, the EU authorized representative is:

Springer Nature Customer Service Center GmbH
Europaplatz 3
69115 Heidelberg, Germany

The manufacturer's authorised representative in the EU is Springer Nature Customer Service Centre GmbH, Europaplatz 3, 69115 Heidelberg, Germany. If you have any concerns regarding our products, please contact ProductSafety@springernature.com

Printed and bound by CPI Group (UK) Ltd, Croydon, CR0 4YY

28/03/2026

02080358-0003